ALL ABOUT...

ELECTRONIC

PERCUSSION

By Mike Snyder

Edited by Robby Berman

Foreword by Johnny Rabb

HAL•LEONARD®

ISBN-13: 978-0-634-05450-1
ISBN-10: 0-634-05450-3

Published by Hal Leonard Corporation
7777 Bluemound Road
P.O. Box 13819
Milwaukee, WI 53213

 Library of Congress Cataloging-in-Publication Data

Snyder, Mike.
  All about-- electronic percussion / by Mike Snyder ; edited by Robby
Berman ; foreword by Johnny Rabb. -- 1st ed.
     p. cm.
  Includes index.
  ISBN-13: 978-0-634-05450-1
  1. Drum machine. 2. Sequencer (Musical instrument) I. Berman, Robby. II. Title.
ML1092.S63 2006
786.9'19--dc22
                                        2006017000

Printed in the U.S.A.

First Edition

Visit Hal Leonard online at
www.halleonard.com

CONTENTS

FOREWORD

by Johnny Rabb

I purchased my first electronic drums around the age of 15. At that time, it was either a car or electronic drums. I chose the drums. (OK, should have gotten the car, I know.) Although I had a keen interest in electronics, the information between the covers of the owner's manual was overwhelming and difficult to retain. Within a year, after being frustrated by the weak sounds and being scared by the manual, the electronic drums were gone, sold with a sigh of relief and resolve. I told myself that from then on, I would play only acoustic drums.

Time marched on. My fascination with electronic music and drums could not be denied any longer. I slowly started collecting an array of samplers, drum machines, and the like, yet I still had the feeling that I was a complete novice. What I didn't know still completely frustrated me. Then I had the pleasure of meeting Mike, the type of person who believes in helping others.

We met at the E-DRUM Expo in Pasadena, sponsored by Roland, in November 2002. In less than a half hour over coffee, he introduced me to many new ideas and concepts regarding music and electronic drums. While co-presenting a clinic/masterclass session the next morning, I witnessed Mike make the seemingly complex mystery of electronic drums clear and easy to understand. By the end of his clinic, I understood things with a clarity I never thought possible. Mike knocked down barriers for me regarding MIDI, triggering, crosstalk, and many other topics I once feared were way over my head. Mike's knowledge is as deep as you can dig, but his approach to teaching is painless. He made it fun—and easy! I soon found myself feeling like an electronic musician (and coffee addict).

Since then, Mike and I have become close friends. I continue to learn with the foundation of knowledge he has given me. Now it's your chance to meet Mike Snyder. Consider *All About Electronic Percussion* your direct connection to your own personal electronic drum and percussion guru. I haven't asked a single question that he hasn't been able to answer. He knows acoustic drums intimately. The same goes for electronics and MIDI. When you hear him perform, you will hear a musician with a full knowledge of his craft. *All About Electronic Percussion* is the most in-depth, easy-to-follow book on electronic drumming you can buy.

Mike, congratulations on a wonderful accomplishment. Thank you for this definitive book on electronic drumming!

—Johnny "Unk J" Rabb

A NOTE FROM
THE AUTHOR

Drums and percussion have been a part of my life for almost as long as I can remember. My first drum set was made from Folgers® coffee cans and scrap wood from my Father's discard pile. Today my home is overrun with drum and percussion instruments. They fill my music studio, garage, and various recording studios around my hometown. I think there is even gear at a few neighbors' houses. I've always had an attraction to the sound of anything I could hit. If I could hit it and it made sound, it had a place in my heart and in my garage. My passion for percussion aside, I truly would like to get both cars in the garage at some point in my life.

My love of sound was highly valuable during my years in Los Angeles as a film and TV drummer and percussionist. At times the sounds I had to produce had very little to do with the instruments of my formal academic training. I mean, how many different pairs of goat nail rattles do you have?

Me? Five. The motto that my percussion teacher and mentor Ken Watson burned into my brain was "I don't care if you have to hang it from the ceiling, put a mallet in your mouth and tape another to your foot, just GET THE SOUND!" These words echo in my head every time I go to perform or record. Get the sound. Do whatever it takes to get the sound. This is some of the best advice I ever received, second only to "Always be on time."

Incorporating drum and percussion electronics into my bag of tricks has helped me in numerous ways. When first marketing myself as a studio drummer and percussionist, it made me much more marketable as player. (We musicians are not very different from a can of soup in that respect.) Like it or not, we are a commodity, and we need to give the person who hired us their money's worth. The addition of the electronics allowed me to offer a bit more, like that free ten pounds you occasionally get in a big bag of kitty litter. The electronics made me more valuable to the person hiring me. You might ask "Why?" Well, it's mostly because I had a vastly-increased sound palette when compared to those players who were using only traditional, acoustic instruments. This was true for both live performing and studio work. Yes, I gave them the extra ten pounds of kitty litter they craved. By the time you're through with this book, you too will be a "bonus bag."

Becoming computer- and electronics-savvy leads to new and easier ways to practice, perform, and record. *All About Electronic Percussion* will demystify the world of electronic drums, MIDI, and computers. It will give you the vocabulary and tools to begin your journey through this exciting area of music and help you to understand it better. After reading *All About Electronic Percussion*, keep it around. It will be a great reference guide.

Let's get going!

Mike Snyder
Drummer, Percussionist, and Electronics Junkie
Portland, Oregon USA
http://mikesnyder.net

ACKNOWLEDGMENTS

I don't quite know where to begin—there are so many people involved, not only with this book, but with my knowledge base and career in general—but begin I will.

Thanks to Bill Katoski and Mario DeCiutiis of KAT and Alternate Mode for their knowledge and friendship, especially in the early days when people were still wondering why we'd even want to play electronics. We've come a long way.

Steve Fisher of Roland, what can I say? You're a great drummer, great guy, and electronic drum visionary. We all should thank you. Our working relationship and personal friendship enriches both my personal and professional life, and has helped change the face of electronic drumming. Thanks for calling after my Trigger Perfect drum trigger days. What a drum team!

Many folks have had major influences along the way: Bob Stark, one of the best recording engineers alive; the great studio percussionist Ken Watson, who taught me so much about sound; Tim Ellis for, among other things, that one recording session where I "became a Rock drummer."

Johnny Rabb, thanks for being a friend and brother. You've rekindled my zeal for drumming. I'm so glad we didn't die that November afternoon in Ohio. Scott Summers, thanks for swerving.

Thanks to Marco Soccoli at Vic Firth, Scott Donnell at DW and PDP Drums and Percussion, Rob Schnell, my friend and Audix connection, Herbie May, Matt Connors, Chris Hart and Michelle Jacoby at Remo, and Steve Fisher and the rest of the drum team at Roland. Thank you all for your continued support and encouragement, as well as your contributions to music as a whole.

To everyone at Roland Japan and Roland Corp US, "Snappy" Katsuda and the entire drum team—Chris Bristol, David Garza, Drew Armentrout, and Mary Ann Sherman. I'm glad you are all there! Robby Berman, thank you for proofing and polishing the text, and generally making everything read better. Paul Youngblood, thanks for the opportunity.

Most of all, my thanks goes to the joy in my life, Maggie Stock. You put up with so much from this kooky husband of yours, everything from being a "road widow" much of the time to my booming voice and stale jokes. How can I repay you? I'm giddy that I get to spend this journey with you.

ONE

ELECTRONIC DRUMS
A Brief History

Reflections on Two Decades

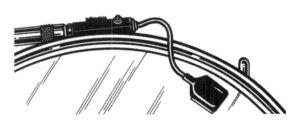

As I gathered the research materials for this chapter, I was struck by how fertile the early days of electronic percussion were. Being closely involved with electronic percussion, both as a player and inventor in those formative days, gave me a very subjective view of those frenzied years. It is only now that I'm beginning to appreciate their importance. In the 1980s, you really had to want to play electronics. The available technology was crude and the pads felt terrible. All the negatives aside, there were reasons for enduring the long hours of troubleshooting—and the arm pain. Today, the fruits of these early labors are all around us.

Many of the early innovators have departed the industry, but have left their permanent mark on the electronic percussion world. Some of us have remained and are working to advance the technology even closer to what we've dreamt about for years. Because of the vision and zeal of countless people over the last few decades, we all now enjoy great-sounding, incredible-feeling, and very expressive electronic drums. It is only going to get better.

The Four Eras of Electronic Percussion

In my examination of the last 50 years or so of electronic drum history, I've identified four distinct eras. The beginning of each of these eras is marked by the introduction of a revolutionary product, usually created by a visionary. The eras have relatively clear beginnings. The products created are eventually accepted into mainstream drumming or morph into even better products and ideas. Think about it: in less than 30 years we've gone from analog electronic drums like the Syndrum—peeewwww, peeewwww—to incredible drum sets like the Roland V-Drums. Awesome times. I love drums.

Ponder this tidbit over that energy drink:
Roland Drums & Percussion is the largest-grossing drum company in the world, not just the largest electronic drum company. Roland has larger gross sales than any other drum company, acoustic and/or electronic.*

As with any emerging technology, determining specific dates for events and products can be a bit difficult. This brief history is meant to serve as an overview of the history of electronic drums and percussion. It is not the definitive word, by far. That being said...

Era One

Begins *c*1949
Rhythm Machine/Drum Machine (non-real-time pre-programmed patterns)

Era Two

Begins *c*1978
Electronic Drums (real-time performance)

Era Three

Begins 1992
Complete Electronic Drum Sets

Era Four

Begins 1997
V-Drums®

*Based on public sales figures for the year 2004.

The Eras: A Closer Look

Era One: Rhythm Machine/Drum Machine

This is the era drummers over the age of 35 love to hate. In this era, the drum machine was created—that little box that put a bunch of drummers out of work. How much the drum machine actually culled the herds of working drummers is open to debate. What it did accomplish was opening the door of technology to drums and percussion.

I had always assumed that the rhythm machine was created in the 1960s. To my surprise and delight, I found a much earlier specimen. It very well might be the first rhythm machine ever created. Fig. 1.1 is two photos of the Musser Maestro Marimba Metron, created by marimba virtuoso Clair Omar Musser c1949. Yes, 1949. Musser used this Rhythm Machine, as he called it, in performances and in his teaching studio at Northwestern University. It uses sounds made with vacuum tube technology, as well as acoustic cymbals struck using solenoid-actuated beaters. The photo to the right in fig. 1.1 shows the Metron opened up, revealing its inner workings.

Fig. 1.1. Metron photos reprinted with the permission of the Percussive Arts Society.

Tip:
The preservation of historically important instruments like this is only a small slice of what the Percussive Arts Society does. Visit their website (http://pas.org) and become a member.

Other notable rhythm machine moments

In 1964, Ikutaro Kakehashi first displayed Ace Electronics products at the NAMM*
tradeshow. Mr. K, as we call him, went on to found Roland Musical Instruments in
1972. Fig. 1.2 shows Mr. K at the 1964 NAMM show next to the R1 Rhythm Ace. This
show started what has become a long career, changing the way all music is made.

Photo: Roland

Fig. 1.2

Rhythm machines remained pretty much the same until 1975. That year, John
Stayton Simonton Jr. of PAiA Electronics created the first user-programmable
rhythm machine, the PAiA Programmable Drum Set. Although not a commercial
success, this programmable analog rhythm machine set the stage for all future
drum machines (see fig. 1.3).

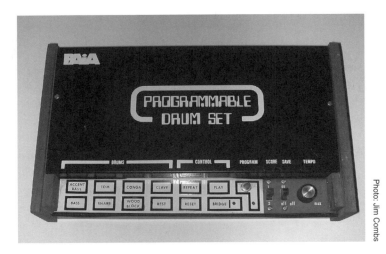

Photo: Jim Combs

Fig. 1.3

NAMM is the common name for the International Music Products Association.

In 1978, Roland—now six years old—released the CR-78 CompuRhythm (see fig. 1.4). This was Roland's first user-programmable rhythm machine. Like the PAiA rhythm machine, the CR-78 was analog, and therefore didn't sound like acoustic drums. The CR-78 reached its height of popularity when Phil Collins used it on the 1981 hit song "In the Air Tonight."

Fig. 1.4

The next two rhythm machines—now more commonly referred to as drum machines—changed the face of music. With the introduction of the Linn Electronics LM-1, the sound of drumming was forever altered. Not only was the user able to program their own patterns, the LM-1 used sampled sounds. It was the first digital drum machine. Drums machines now sounded closer to acoustic drums, not just electronic representations of the same. The LM-1 (see fig. 1.5) was introduced *c*1979. Its big brother, the Linn 9000 (see fig. 1.6), was introduced in 1984. In the 1980s, the Linn 9000 was a recording studio staple.

Fig. 1.5

Fig. 1.6

Linn photos reprinted with the permission of Jim Rivers of Audio Playground.
http://Keyboardmuseum.org

There were other great drum machines in the '80s. Around 1984, Oberheim had the DMX and DX drum machines. These machines had an astounding 64K of sample memory—64K for all the sounds! At the time, a songwriter neighbor of mine, Alex Armstrong, had a *DX* drum machine on which I frequently programmed patterns for his song demos. Other drum machines at the time were E-mu Systems' Drumulator in 1983, and Roland's *TR-808* in 1980 (see fig. 1.7). Although the TR-808 was not a huge commercial success when first released, its low second-hand price and cool analog sounds made it the drum machine to use in the early days of Hip Hop and Dance music. Today, it is still one of the most sought-after drum machines.

Fig. 1.7

The next generation of drum machines became much more powerful, both in features and quality/quantity of samples. The Roland R-8 Rhythm Composer (see fig. 1.8) and the Alesis HR-16—both introduced in 1988—were the models for all drum machines to come. The Roland *R-8* was my first drum machine. The later rack-mount version, the R-8M, is still in my rack today.

Fig. 1.8

Drum machines have now taken the next logical step in their evolution, the transition from being hardware-based to being software-based. Products like FXpansion's BFD, and Propellerheads' Reason software are leading drumming into the computer age. All you drummers out there need to spend time working on your mouse chops, too!

Tidbit:
The present-day company Digidesign started existence as Digidrums.
They were a source of third-party sounds blown into EPROM chips
for use in some of the early drum machines and electronic drums.

Era Two: Electronic Drums/Real-Time Performance*

This era is very near and dear to my heart because it was during this time that I began my heavy involvement with drum electronics, both as a player in the studios of Los Angeles and as a designer. In the late 1980s, I worked with Bill Katoski of Kat on the drum triggering portion of the drumKAT. I founded my company, Trigger Perfect Drum Triggers, in 1987. Just a few years later, we were the largest producer of acoustic drum triggers in the world. We manufactured triggers not only under our own nameplate, but for Kat and Roland as well.

Some of the influential names of the time, with their associated products and/or companies: Joe Pollard, Syndrum; Dave Kusek, Synare; Bill Katoski, MalletKAT and DrumKAT; Dave Simmons, Simmons; Glynn Thomas, Simmons; Dan Dauz, Dauz Designs; Tom Henry, Drum Tech; Reek Havok (drum triggering pioneer); Hand Nordelious, ddrum; and Darrell Johnson of Axis.

The first two companies to make real-time performance a possibility were Pollard International and Star Instruments. They made what are commonly believed to be the first electronic drums—and man, did they sound electronic! Although they made other models of drums, the two single-drum products were, respectively, the Syndrum CM (see fig. 1.9), and the Synare 3 (see fig. 1.10). These products were introduced *c*1976–78. Their analog sound became the rage. The list of artists using the Syndrum read like a who's who of drumming.

Fig. 1.9

Photo: Drew Armentrout

Fig. 1.10

The advances of the early days of electronic drums were made possible by a huge group of people. Please forgive if I have missed anyone.

The Brits Land in the US... Again

The electronic drums that shook the drumming world came from England *c*1982, the Simmons SDSV. This set of drums, with its hexagonal pads and fat analog sounds, created the desire to explore electronic drums in an entire generation of players. I was one of those inspired players. This kit caught the attention of the likes of Bill Bruford, Harvey Mason, and "Texas" Tim Root. Fig. 1.11 shows "Texas" Tim Root *c*1985 with the next generation of Simmons Drums, the *SDS7*. The first hybrid analog/digital set of drums. My first full set of electronic drums was the Simmons SDS9 kit. The SDS9 had MIDI capability. I didn't quite know what I needed MIDI for, but I knew it was cool!

Photo: Tim Root

Fig. 1.11

In 1985, Roland released their DDR-30 Digital Drums. The triangular-shaped PD-10 and PD-20 had, as did all the other manufacturers, a real space-age look. Fig. 1.12 shows Tim Root seated at Roland DDR-30 drums before one of his many clinics for Simmons. Fig. 1.13 is photo of the front face of a DDR-30 drum module.

Fig. 1.12

Fig. 1.13

These instruments gave way to a flood of innovation. It seemed like around every corner there was another company coming out with a new electronic drum set. After entering into the market with the ddrumPlus! in 1985, ddrum released the ddrum2 in 1986. The ddrum2 sounded like acoustic drums and used acoustic drumheads on its pads. The ddrum2 saw wide use, both live and in the recording studio.

Even the acoustic drum manufacturers tried their hand at electronic drums. Tama released their Techstar electronic drums in 1984, quickly followed in 1985 by the TechstarII drums. Yamaha introduced their EPS-D8 electronic drums in 1987. Drum Workshop even distributed Dynacord electronic drums, and in 1984 released the EP-1 electronic trigger pedal based on their popular DW5000 kick pedal.

Pearl had had the Syncussion, a Syndrum-like percussion synthesizer, in their product line since 1979. They added the five-piece Drum-X in 1985 and the vastly expanded Syncussion-X in 1986 (see fig. 1.14). With cymbal sounds in the sound module and pads designed to be dedicated cymbal pads, the Syncussion-X was ahead of its time.

Photo: Pearl Corporation. Special thanks to Gene Okamoto

Fig. 1.14

Pad and Accessory Manufacturers

During this time, there were smaller companies and individuals that helped shape the future of electronic drumming. Manufacturers of individual pads and accessories abounded.

Dauz Designs pioneered electronic drum pad design. Dan Dauz continues to design products. There are still many Dauz Pads in use today.

Larry Shamus of S&S Industries created many innovative drum pads throughout the 1980s and 1990s. After Larry's death, his brother Mike Shamus carried on the legacy of S&S Industries. My company, Trigger Perfect Drum Triggers, was sold to Mike in the late 1990s.

Peter Hart, of Hart Dynamics, continues to develop and sell pads to this day.

Fig. 1.15

Tom Henry of Drum Tech still develops and sells innovative drum products, both acoustic and electronic. Drum Tech's two-zone pad, the PoleKAT, is one of my all-time-favorite pad designs (see fig. 1.15). This two-zone pad was one of the first uses of FSR film in an individual drum pad.

Acoustic Drum Triggers

Acoustic drum trigger technology was also advancing during this time. Early work on triggering acoustic drums by Reek Havok, Dieter Kaudel of K&K Sound Systems, as well as my work at Trigger Perfect, helped drummers do the near-impossible—trigger electronics from their acoustic drums. Fig. 1.16 shows the very first drum trigger from Trigger Perfect (the DT-1) and its companion passive sensitivity control box, both developed in 1986. The Trigger Perfect SC-10 is shown in fig. 1.17. In 1987, miniaturization allowed for the sensitivity control to be placed in the jack of each individual trigger. 1993 saw the introduction of the patented Trigger Perfect SC-210 (fig. 1.18). It had replaceable parts and a built-in sensitivity control, as well as the ability to adjust how much pressure the trigger element placed on the head. These features have influenced many later acoustic drum trigger designs.

Fig. 1.16

Fig. 1.17

Fig. 1.18

Drum Pad and Mallet Controllers

In 1985, the first drum pad controller was introduced—the Roland Octapad (see fig. 1.19). The Octapad had no internal sounds; it was purely a MIDI controller. The key word here is MIDI. (OK, I know... technically, it's an acronym.) The acceptance of the MIDI specification by the major manufacturers paved the way for the future

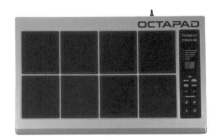

Fig. 1.19

of the drum pad controller. With a drum pad controller, a MIDI cord, and a sound module that was MIDI-capable, the drummer's way of working was forever changed. It was now possible to play a live gig or studio session with a setup no larger than a medium-sized suitcase. The Octapad changed the path of my drumming career. Fig. 1.20 shows me packing up after a gig. The rack in the background contains, among other things, two Akai S900 digital samplers and a Simmons SDS9 tucked in a drawer at the bottom. That rack quickly grew twice as big. My initial dollar investment was huge, well over $40,000 USD. An Octapad controlled it all! By comparison, I would have the same power—actually more—with just two pieces of gear: the Roland HandSonic HPD-15 and the SPD-S sample pad. These two pieces have total street prices of less than $1,500 USD. Boy, I wish I had put some of that gear money into the stock market!

Fig. 1.20

Enter the Beast: KAT

Bill Katoski, after leaving Star Instruments where he worked on the Synare—then owned by Mattel after their purchase of Star Instruments—founded KAT. Bill was able to leave Mattel with his intellectual property—bad for Mattel, good for the drum world. During his time at Star Instruments and Mattel, Bill was developing a hybrid digital/analog mallet instrument. Mattel got cold feet and jettisoned the project, says Mario DeCiutiis, former KAT VP, and now owner of KAT technology marketed under the Alternate Mode name. Dave Samuels played this early instrument and is *still* playing it, according to Mario.

The original analog MalletKAT was abandoned in favor of a MIDI-controller style mallet instrument, using the new technology of MIDI (see fig. 1.21). It was introduced at PASIC (Percussive Arts Society International Convention) in 1986. Interesting to note is that Simmons introduced their Silicon Mallet instrument at this same show. Both of these instruments were some of the first uses of FSR (force sensing resisters) in electronic drums and percussion. The MalletKAT was the core MIDI controller in my recording studio setup in the late 1980s and early 1990s.

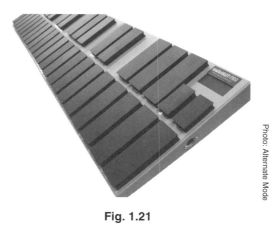

Fig. 1.21

Photo: Alternate Mode

In 1988, KAT brought the sensitivity and aftertouch capabilities of FSR to the world of drum controllers in the form of the drumKAT. This Mickey-Mouse-looking piece of gear (see fig. 1.22) offered—and still does—great sensitivity and incredibly advanced MIDI implementation. My first drumKAT was serial number 00004. It served me well for over a decade. The contributions of Bill Katoski, Mario DeCiutiis, and the rest of the KAT team were invaluable.

Fig. 1.22

Photo: Alternate Mode

Era Three: Complete Electronic Drum Sets

While Pearl seemed to be on the right path to making a complete electronic drum set, the Syncussion-X still lacked some of the most basic drum set functions, most notably smooth open-to-closed hi-hat sounds and chokeable cymbals. Enter the Roland TDE-7K Compact Drum System. In 1992, Roland's long involvement in electronic percussion gave the drumming world its first complete electronic drum set. Steve Fisher—now head of the Roland US Drum and Percussion Division—is shown here in the early 1990s with the TDE-7K drum set (see fig. 1.23). This drum set blazed the path for the revolutionary drum products yet to come from Roland's worldwide drum and percussion development team. During this time, Steve Fisher became the pied piper of electronic drum technology, setting up, demonstrating, and tearing down the TDE-7K with the zeal of a man possessed.

Photo: Roland Corp US

Fig. 1.23

The Roland development team had created a revolutionary product. A few of the people from Roland Japan critical to bringing these drums to market were Masato Katsuda and Mr. Yamashita. Masato Katsuda—"Snappy," as we call him—continues to be an integral part of the Roland development team. Fig. 1.24 is from January 2001, with Snappy in his iconic thumbs-up pose. Fig. 1.25 shows Snappy with other members of the Roland drum team from around the world.

Fig. 1.24

Fig. 1.25. Back (left to right): Hiroyuki Nishi, Masato "Snappy" Katsuda, and me, Mike Snyder. Front (left to right): Steve Fisher, David Garza, Tommy Snyder, Johnny Rabb, and Michael Schack.

Roland added a few other drum sets and percussion controllers over the next five years, steadily building their drum business. Although the trends of popular music at the time dampened some of the acceptance of electronic drums, no one was prepared for what was coming. The V-Drum era was about to be unleashed on the world. The entire drumming paradigm was about to be irreversibly altered. Dramatic words, to be sure, but it was going to be a dramatic change.

:::::::: Era Four: V-Drums

On January 16, 1997, the drumming world changed. This was the date Roland unveiled the V-Pro TD-10 V-Drum Kit to the world at the Winter NAMM Show in Anaheim, California (see fig. 1.26). This drum set addressed many of the playability issues drummers had with earlier electronic drums. They were quiet. The V-Pro kit used new, two-ply mesh head technology that made the pads tuneable for feel. The sound quality of the TD-10 sound module was incredible! Snare drum and ride cymbal sounds even changed timbre as you played in different areas of the pad.

Fig. 1.26

All these new features paled when compared to user interface for editing the drum kits. The TD-10 used pictures. The COSM (Composite Object Sound Modeling) technology Roland had been pioneering for years had finally made its way into electronic drums. Lucky us. Acoustic drum parameters were used to edit the TD-10's kits—no more electronic terminology to frighten and confuse. The user simply had to chose from very familiar items: head type, shell depth, and how much duct tape to use to muffle the drum.

My first set of V-Pro V-Drums arrived in September 1997. I credit this set of drums, in part, for rekindling my waning interest in drumming.

Fig. 1.27

The next big step in electronic drum playability came in 2001 with the introduction of a complete line of V-Cymbals (see fig. 1.27). For me, the V-Cymbals were the missing link. Electronic drums had arrived.

Fig. 1.28

I must mention here the introduction of the Roland HandSonic HPD-15 hand percussion controller in 2000. This was the first percussion controller designed specifically with the hand drummer in mind. This piece of gear is a must-have for all percussionists (see fig. 1.28).

The V-Pro TD-20S drum set—the second-generation flagship V-Drum set from Roland—was released in January 2004. This drum set was almost a complete redesign from its predecessor, right down to a new sound set for the TD-20 drum module. Fig. 1.29 shows me playing a V-Pro TD-20S drum set during a clinic at Grandma's Music in Albuquerque, New Mexico in early 2005. Also introduced at this time were the VH-12 two-piece hi-hat cymbals (see fig. 1.30). These cymbals mount on the drummer's hi-hat stand of choice and offer unequalled expressiveness and sensitivity.

Fig. 1.29

Stay tuned for more cool stuff!

There you have it, a brief history of electronic drums. There are more great innovations coming. Hang on!

Fig. 1.30

TWO

CREATIVE USE OF ELECTRONIC DRUMS

:::::: "This is not your father's drum set."

For many drummers, the world of electronic drums—and music technology in general—is a mysterious place filled with things they've never before dealt with. Concepts and ways of working can be different from previous experiences. In addition to playing the drums, the modern drummer is also part drum tech, computer geek, and recording engineer. Rest assured, the new concepts and tools electronic drums offer can make practice, performance, and recording better, easier, and more focused. If you make your living as a musician, it will make you a more salable commodity. Embracing technology has defined and directed my music career in ways I've never imagined.

Practice, Rehearsal, Performance, and Recording

Practice

I think the overriding reason people purchase electronic drums is for practice. Electronic drums have a great many advantages over acoustic drum sets: they're quiet, they have many different sounding kits, they have a built-in metronome, you can record your playing on most, you can play along with "tracks." They're just plain fun!

The Volume Knob

Hands down, the volume knob is the best feature on electronic drums. Once you put on the headphones and turn the up the headphone volume, you're in your own little drum heaven. You can practice at most anytime of the day or night—without disturbing your kids, parents, neighbors, spouse, or even Fido. Having electronic drums can dramatically increase the time you spend practicing. Hopefully, this will translate into an improvement in your playing.

Dozens of Different Drum Sets

The importance of having different sounding drum sets available is often overlooked. You see, the sound we get from a drum set is directly tied to *what* we play on the drums, as well as *how well* we play them. Think about this: a drummer's first drum set has traditionally been an inexpensive kit, with an entry-level set of cymbals. Poor quality heads often make the kit sound awful, but at least the drummer doesn't know how to tune them. On this drum set, the drummer is expected to practice many different styles of drumming—from Funk to Rock to Jazz. There's no way just one drum set can serve as the sole practice instrument for all these different styles. Each style requires different sounding drums. Enter the electronic drum set. If you want to practice your Rock licks, you can select a big-sounding drum set, complete with effects like reverb. The next moment you can switch to a small, high-pitched Bebop kit complete with ringy kick drum. What a great enhancement to your practice routine.

The Sequencer

The onboard sequencer is an invaluable tool. You can play along with music (also called "backing tracks"). The music you're hearing is not recorded audio, but rather sequenced performance data used to play backing instrument sounds that are inside the drum module. Because it is performance data, the tempo can be changed without changing the music's pitch. How spiffy is that?

Another way to use the sequencer is to record your practicing and then play it back. As with the backing tracks, your practicing is recorded as performance data, not audio. Therefore the tempo can be slowed down to hear in detail how you're playing. Further enhancing this feature is the ability to add in the metronome click as a reference. This use of the sequencer is a tool I constantly utilize in my practice routine. I wish I'd had it 30 years ago.

The "Mix In"

If you want to play along with your favorite bands, you can plug an audio source (CD, MP3 player, etc.) directly into the drum module. The audio will be mixed in with the audio from the drum module.

The Rhythm Coach

A few years back, Roland introduced a new way to practice. It was the Rhythm Coach. The Rhythm Coach combines an advanced metronome, mesh-head technology, onboard drum and percussion sounds (on some models like the RMP-1 and RMP-5), and unique Rhythm Coach exercises into a sleek package. Fig. 2.1 shows the RMP-5 expanded with an optional kick pad and cymbal. Johnny Rabb calls this combination the most complete portable practice tool he's ever experienced. Go, Johnny! With the Rhythm Coach, you have the perfect practice partner. It'll check your time, score how accurately you can play with the metronome, help you with odd subdivisions of the beat, and never complain.

Fig. 2.1

You have to check it out.

Rehearsal

How cool would it be to have band practice and walk away with your ears not ringing? Rehearsals often take place in rooms much too small for the music being played. With electronic drums, the band's volume will no longer be governed by the acoustic drums. Just adjust the volume to the desired level and hit the electronic drums as hard as you want. Use rehearsals as a time to learn new material, create new arrangements, and otherwise perfect music—without making an enemy of the lead singer.

Now all we have to do is convince guitar players to back off the volume.

Performance

Electronic Drums Only

Drum sounds are an integral part of today's music. Change the drum sound too much, and the music may not sound as good. With electronic drums, you can change drum sets as frequently as desired. You can have vastly different sounding kits from tune to tune—or even within a tune—with the touch of a finger. It's also easy to get great drum sounds without using any mics. By plugging the electronic drums directly into the sound system, there won't be any live drum mics for the band to bleed into, or for the person doing sound to mess up.

Hybrid Electronics/Acoustics

The hybrid setup gives the player the best of both worlds—the beloved look and feel of their acoustics and the increased sound palate offered by electronics. Fig. 2.2 shows my setup from the 2003 SoundLab tour sponsored by Roland and DW. The acoustic drums are triggering the TD-8 drum module, producing a huge sound. In addition, the various pads within the drum set can access any sounds in the TD-8 and SPD-20. The SPD-S Sample Pad contains short percussion and bass loops, as well as complete songs to perform with—some are over six minutes long.

Fig. 2.2

Recording

The hardware and software for recording has changed dramatically over the past ten years. It is possible to get high-quality recording, once available only in high-recording studios, in your home. Because of this change, much of today's recording takes place in small production studios. Generally, the layout of these studios is not designed to handle an acoustic drum set. In this situation, electronic drums are the only option. Not only can we get great drum sounds, but our drum performance can be recorded as well, both as MIDI and audio. This is an enormous advantage. If any of the drum sounds need to be changed later on, we don't have to come back and re-record our part. The engineer just dials in another sound using the MIDI data from our original drum performance.

A slightly different setup is commonly used in larger acoustic-drum-friendly studios. The drummer will play triggered acoustic drums instead of pads, and use acoustic cymbals. In addition to the MIDI performance and triggered drum sound from the drum module, the entire drum set's acoustic sound is also recorded—i.e., snare, toms, kick, and overheads. At mix-down, there is an amazing amount of sonic material to choose from to create the perfect-sounding drum tracks. This method of tracking drums is more common than you might think. Many a drum track consists of an acoustic sound beefed up, or completely replaced, by a triggered sound. Electronics have now become another tool we are expected to have in order to do our job as drummers.

THREE

ELECTRONIC DRUM COMPONENTS

Essential to learning any new technology is the understanding of the terminology used to describe it. Using the same definitions allows us all to start at a common point. This chapter will present the definitions for the parts that make up electronic drums: cables, pads, and two major features of drum modules—the trigger inputs and the makeup of the sounds themselves.

We drummers have always dealt with parts—nuts, bolts, tension rods, washers, spurs, etc. I personally like this aspect of drumming. It's very hands-on. In describing acoustic drum parts, we all use relatively common terms. Walk into a drum shop, pretty much anywhere in the world, and ask for a six-mm tension rod or a drop-clutch, and you know what you're going to get. The same is true for electronics. To understand this more easily, we need to learn a little of the terminology up front. Don't freak out if you can't absorb all this new information right away. There's a glossary in the back of this book for future reference. OK, now on to learning about the individual components of electronic drums: the different types of cables, pads, and drum module basics.

The Cables that Connect the Pads

The cable part of electronic drums is quite easy. Two types of cables connect almost every pad to a drum module: the shielded, mono 1/4" male cable (same as a guitar uses), and the shielded, stereo 1/4" male cable (see fig. 3.1). There is also the occasional use of a cable called an insert cable, which I'll cover later in this chapter.

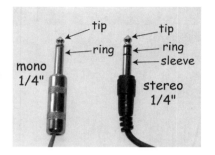

Fig. 3.1

Common Types of Pads

Pad design and technology have come a long, long way since electronic drums were first introduced. In less than 20 years we've gone from pads that looked like a stop sign, and felt like a laminate countertop, to multi-ply, tunable, mesh-headed pads that feel very much like acoustic drums. (Dare I say, perhaps better?). Electronic drum technology, like the rest of computer technology, has improved by quantum leaps. In 25 years, we've gone from Simmons drums to the incredible sound and feel of the Roland V-Pro Series TD-20S drums that were released in January 2004. For me, these technological advancements have helped make it a great time to be a drummer and percussionist. As we go through these next chapters, I hope you'll understand electronic drums even better and learn new ways to use this technology to improve your performing and practicing.

There are three basic kinds of pads: rubber, tunable mesh, and cymbal pads. Roland's two-ply mesh-headed pads and VH-12 hi-hat cymbals might just be the two most important advances in pad technology to date. There are many choices within these three different types of pads, both in manufacturer and features. In addition to construction and feel differences, pads can also have multiple types of trigger technology built into them, giving them the ability to play more than one sound. As of now one-, two-, and three-zone trigger pads are most common. They're known as single trigger, dual trigger, and three-way triggering. You will sometimes see them sometimes referred to as single zone, two zone, and three zone.

Before looking at the specifics of each of the pad types, let's have a look at how pads work in general. It will give us a better foundation to draw upon later when we discuss the specifics of each type of pad.

∷∷∷ How Do Pads Sense a Hit?

The vast majority of pads use piezo sensors (see fig. 3.2) to detect hits on the pad. Piezos give off voltage when they vibrate—in our case, when they're hit. The harder the hit, the more voltage that is given off. Piezos have many different uses outside of drum pads. We most often see (or hear) them used as speakers in electronic gadgets like microwave ovens and pretty much anything else that beeps. Piezos vibrate when voltage is applied to them. They are useful little guys. Pads based on piezos can be used with any drum module on the market.

Fig. 3.2

The graph in fig. 3.3 plots the voltage from a pad hit. The voltage at the peak of this particular waveform (trigger pulse) is about 4.5 volts, which represents a relatively hard hit. The basic voltage used by a drum module to denote soft-to-loud hits ranges from zero to five volts. Using the trigger pulse shown, the sound from the drum module will be loud in volume.

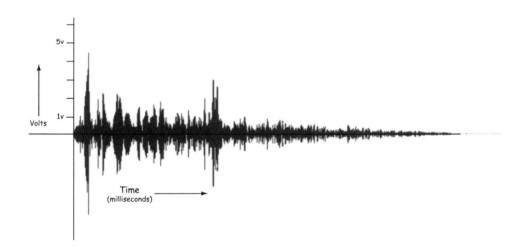

Fig. 3.3. The height of the waveform in a graph shows the sound's amplitude, which translates into its volume.

As you see in fig. 3.4, a lighter hit will produce a smaller amplitude (waveform height) and softer volume from the drum module.

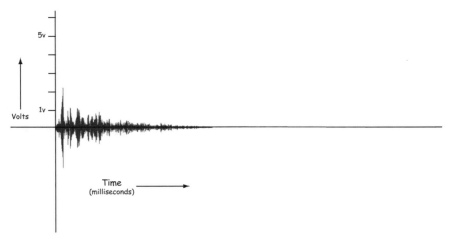

Fig. 3.4

The zero-to-five-volts range for pads is only a guideline (an unwritten one, too). Drum modules and trigger interfaces differ from model to model and from manufacturer to manufacturer. The gain or sensitivity setting on a drum module or trigger interface is there to adjust these differences.

Don't obsess about having to deal with these differences, because the default settings on plug and play electronic drums will be adequate for almost everyone's needs. In fact, when using Roland drums, I have had to alter the factory defaults only in rare instances.

For a more in-depth discussion of the subtleties of how pads sense being struck, read chapter eleven, "Triggering from Acoustic Drums."

Pad Designs: Rubber Pads, Mesh Heads and Cymbal Pads

The Rubber Pad: Varieties Abound

Let's look at the venerable rubber pad. It's hard to track down exactly who made the first rubber pad and when, but by the mid-1980s there were many small startup companies designing, manufacturing, and selling them. The list included small companies like Dauz Designs, larger companies  like Roland, and even acoustic drum companies like Tama and Pearl. It was very exciting to be involved in a completely new area of drumming. At that time, there was just a handful of us designing, using, and evangelizing electronic drum technology. We helped shape the future.

Basically, rubber pads come in two flavors: single trigger and dual-trigger. The technology used in most single-trigger rubber pads is pretty much the same. There are some differences between the types of technology used in dual-trigger pads, with two types of designs being used—true dual-trigger pads and membrane-switching pads.

True Dual-trigger Pads

True dual-trigger pads use two piezos, generally one to trigger the head and one to trigger the rim. Although a few dual-trigger rubber pads are built this way, most true dual-trigger pads have mesh heads. These include those from PinTech and those from Roland, the first to put tunable mesh heads on electronic drums. More on mesh pads a little later.

Membrane-Switching Pads

Membrane-switching pads have been around since c1992, when they were introduced in the Roland TDE-7K drum set. This design changed everything. It used one piezo on the head of the pad to trigger both the head and the rim. The secret was the use of a material called FSR, for Force Sensing Resistors. FSR detects pressure, not vibration like a piezo, and is used on the rim of the pad. Fig. 3.5 is an exploded view of a Roland PD-7 pad. The single piezo can be seen mounted to the steel plate on the underside of the pad's rubber playing

Fig. 3.5

surface, and I'm pinching the FSR between my thumb and forefinger. As you can see, the FSR is a thin, flexible piece of plastic. A membrane-switching pad, like the one shown, can function in three different ways:

1. When you hit the center of the pad, it acts just like any other single-trigger piezo pad. Because of this, it can be used in any drum module.

2. To play the rim, you hit the rim and the center of the pad at the same time. You see, the single piezo also works for the rim. There's a circuit in the drum module that detects that the rim membrane is pressed (by the rim shot), and the module knows to send the sound for the rim. In order to use the rim trigger on this type of pad, a drum module has to be designed to have this special circuit (see fig. 3.6).

Fig. 3.6

3. The genius of using FSR is that it makes it possible for us to choke cymbals, just like our acoustics. Because the FSR in the rim senses pressure, there is a circuit in the drum module that senses that the rim has been pinched, so it chokes off any sound playing that was triggered by the pad's head or rim (see fig. 3.7). I'd like to buy a cup of coffee for the guy who came up with this idea.

Fig. 3.7

All Roland drum modules and percussion pads (except the older SPD-6, which doesn't have pad inputs) accept membrane-switching pads… dual-trigger heaven. To this day, some 15 years after the introduction of the choking electronic cymbal, people are still amazed that you can choke the cymbals. There are always lots of wide eyes and surprised looks.

Membrane-switching technology is also used in dual and three-way trigger cymbal pads. We'll cover those later in the chapter.

How Do Rubber Pads Feel?

From a playability standpoint, older rubber pads all have similar performance characteristics. This changed in 2004 with the introduction of the Roland PD-8 dual-trigger pad. This newer pad has greatly improved the rubber pad's reputation by being more responsive to soft playing than older rubber pads were, and by having a much better stick feel. The rubber compound used on the playing surface is just the right mixture of soft and hard rubber. All of the drum modules with which I've used the pad respond quickly and accurately, even when playing soft, multiple-bounce rolls. All this is a vast improvement over prior pads. And remember, it's dual trigger (membrane-switching) and very affordable.

TIP:
When buying additional pads, even if you have an older drum module that isn't compatible with membrane-switching pads (such as an Alesis D-series module), buy membrane-switching pads anyway. They'll work as single-trigger pads, and this way you'll already have dual-trigger pads when you decide to upgrade your drum module to one that's compatible.

Mesh Pads

In 1997, Roland introduced the two-ply mesh heads (see fig. 3.8), the greatest advance to date in the feel of electronic drum pads. This was such a large leap forward that Roland was able to get a US patent on the design. Finally we had a pad that, one could argue, felt just as good as our acoustics. Mesh pads have great response and sensitivity and are tunable. This proved to me that Roland designs and builds drums with professional drummer and consumer input.

Fig. 3.8

Eureka! Nirvana! The clouds lifted and the sun, after years of gloom, was finally shining brightly on the world of electronic drums. All was good.

Like rubber pads, mesh pads come in single- and dual-trigger models. Dual-trigger mesh pads are true dual-trigger pads and can have different sounds assigned to the head and the rim. True dual-trigger pads like the Roland PD-80R, 105, 120, and 125 (see fig. 3.9, which shows a Roland PD-120) work in the snare drum inputs of the TD-3, 6, 6V, 8, and TD-10, but none of their other inputs. Most of these other inputs are membrane-switching only. I must add, however, that Roland's newest high-end drum module, the TD-20, can use true dual-trigger pads in almost every input—and there are 15 inputs. With that many inputs, you could replicate an Octa-Plus set of lore…

This Season, Layering Is In

You'll see a number of different manufacturers making mesh pads, but they're single-ply heads, while Roland's are two-ply and made of a mesh material exclusive to Roland. Play both types. I'm sure you'll prefer the feel of the two-ply heads because they don't have the trampoline-like feel of the single-ply heads.

Fig. 3.9

Durability is an aspect of the mesh-headed pad design that doesn't get a lot of attention. The design of the mesh V-Pad's sensor assembly includes an ingenious trigger assembly, a foam cone placed between the head and the piezo sensor. This cushions the piezo crystal, which is inherently fragile, against the stick hit. Fig. 3.9 shows the typical mesh pad sensor arrangement (true dual-trigger).

Cymbal Pads

Cymbal pad design has come a long way in the last few years. We now have, thanks to Roland, cymbal pads that feel, respond, and move like acoustic cymbals. There have been electronic drum pads that have tried to mimic acoustic, but none have come close to the Roland CY & VH-Series cymbal pads. What makes them so special is the attention paid to feel and the way the cymbal pad moves.

Fig. 3.10

The main reason these pads feel so good is that they have a mass similar to acoustic cymbals. They also can be adjusted so that they have the swing of acoustic cymbals. Most crash cymbals of this type are dual trigger (bow and edge) and are chokeable. The main exceptions to this are ride cymbal pads like the Roland CY-15R. The CY-15R is a triple trigger pad, bell, bow, and edge. It too is chokeable as well (see fig. 3.10).

The acoustic cymbal model is carried to near perfection in the Roland VH-12 hi-hats (see fig. 3.11). They mount to an acoustic hi-hat stand, and they open and close. Almost too cool for words!

Fig. 3.11

Kick Drum Pad Types

Like snare and tom pads, kick pads can be separated into the basic rubber and mesh-headed variety. They can then further be divided into upright designs that are similar to an acoustic kick drum, and those that have affectionately become known as reverse beater designs. Both have been around since the beginning days of electronic drums, although the first upright kick pads where sort of like playing a laminate countertop. This wasn't very good for sticks, and felt even worse with a pedal and beater. Those days are gone, thankfully, and virtually all modern kick pads feel infinitely better. The decision as to kick pad type is one of personal preference. With that in mind, let's look at some of the available options.

Reverse Beater Kick Pads

I personally designed the miniKick reverse beater kick drum pad for KAT some 15 years ago, so I have to confess I lean a great deal toward liking this design. The KD-7 is a kick pad of similar design that Roland currently makes. Fig. 3.12 shows the miniKick and KD-7 side by side. This basic design has been around forever and is very reliable. Reverse beater pads, although not offering the great feel of mesh-headed pads, are compact and easy to pack up and haul around. I always carry one to use with my HandSonic set up because carrying an upright pad would be too bulky. This type of kick pad is a great compact option for all percussion pad setups.

Fig. 3.12

You don't have to use the KD-7 only as a kick drum pad (see fig. 3.13). I often use it to the left of my hi-hat pedal to play left-foot clave patterns. It's a humbling thing to do!

Fig. 3.13

Upright Rubber Kick Pads

Even though there have been upright (vertical) rubber kick drum pads in the past, none have, until recently, captured the smack of the kick beater against the drumhead. The Roland KD-8 does just that (see fig. 3.14). It has the feel one associates with a kick drum, including the slap and fatness. It feels great and it's inexpensive. You'll see a lot more of these pads in the future.

Fig. 3.14

The V-Mesh Kick Pad (Yes, it's upright, too.)

The KD-120 gives the look and feel of an acoustic kick drum (see fig. 3.15). Its mass gives it a solid feel with just the right amount of "give" to the head. Like all mesh pads, it's tuneable.

Fig. 3.15

The Module and Types of Trigger Inputs

On a drum module, the jacks you plug pads into are called trigger inputs. You might also hear them referred to simply as inputs. Either way, they do the same thing—use the trigger pulse from the pad to make the internal sounds play. The received signal is also used to generate the MIDI data that is sent out the MIDI output.

The various types of trigger inputs available on drum modules can be broken down into five different types: single trigger, membrane switching (dual trigger), true dual trigger, dual mono, and edge (used for three-way triggering cymbal pads). All of these inputs work slightly differently from one another, and each accepts different pad types. Although it may seem like a bit of a quagmire, you'll understand it all by the end of this chapter. That is, if you read it all…

1. Single-Trigger Inputs

The single-trigger input is not found on many modern drum modules. It was used extensively on older drum modules like the Alesis D-4 and DM-Pro. With single-trigger inputs, no matter what type of pad or type of cable you use (dual-trigger pads require a stereo cable), the pad will function only as a single-trigger pad, meaning only one sound at a time can be assigned to the head of the pad.

Most of the drum modules made before the 1992 introduction of the Roland TD-7 sound module had only single-trigger inputs. At the time, there weren't many dual-trigger pads available. Roland had a quad-trigger pad on its DDR-30 drum set (the PD-31), but it needed a lot of cables and a lot of inputs. Dauz Designs also had a dual-trigger pad, but with that you had to use a Y-cable and two inputs to make it work as dual trigger with most drum modules. The Roland TD-7 sound module changed all that, since it had nine dual-trigger inputs and pads with which you could choke cymbals.

TIP:
In my opinion, older trigger modules like the Alesis D-Series, and even the Roland PM-16 (no sounds, just a trigger-to-MIDI interface) may seem like a good deal. But beware. Like computer power, the technology used to power drum modules is constantly increasing. The Roland TMC-6 is a modern trigger-to-MIDI interface (no sounds) that has lightning-fast triggering and is dual-trigger- and hi-hat controller-compatible. Consider using it if you need an interface without sounds. It works well with all pads, rubber or mesh, and even with acoustic drum triggers.

2. Membrane-Switching Inputs

The most common type of input on current drum modules is the membrane-switching, dual-trigger input. This type of input will work only with membrane-switching pads like Roland's PD-7, PD-8, and PD-9s, as well as the CY-6, CY-8, CY-12RC/C, CY-12H, CY-14C, and CY-15-RC. True dual-trigger pads like Roland's PD-125 and PD-105 will not function as dual-trigger pads in these inputs, but will work great as single-trigger pads. OK, this is where a blanket statement like the last one might cause some confusion. This is because newer drum modules, like Roland's TD-20, now have inputs that are designed to accept both membrane-switching, dual-trigger pads like the PD-8, and true dual-trigger pads like the PD-85, the PD-105, and the PD-125.

3. True Dual-Trigger Inputs

True dual-trigger inputs allow for the use of pads that are designed with two piezo elements. Roland's PD-120, PD-125, and PD-105 pads are true dual-trigger pads. As we saw earlier in the discussion on pads, one is for the head and the other is for the rim. Using a stereo cable, they plug into a single-trigger input, but you still get two sounds from the pad. This type of pad requires the use of a stereo cable from the pad to the module. If a mono cable (guitar cable) is mistakenly used, the pad will be able to trigger only from the head. If your rim trigger doesn't work, check and see if you've made this mistake. Don't feel bad—I've done the same thing.

4. The Edge Input

Three-way triggering cymbals (at the time of this writing, mainly the ride cymbal) require the use of two cables (stereo) and two inputs to work properly (see fig. 3.16). One is used for the bell and the bow of the cymbal and the other is used for the edge sound and cymbal choking. Of course, this means there must be two outputs on the cymbal

Fig. 3.16

pad. A drum module must be capable of three-way triggering for the three-zone ride to function properly. As of this writing, the TDW-1 expanded TD-10, the TD-12, and the TD-20 modules are capable of three-way triggering. I think it's reasonable to believe that there will be other modules in the future which support this feature.

5. Dual-Mono Input

Think of dual-mono input as two independent single-trigger inputs contained in one jack. I assume this input design configuration saves precious real estate by not using two separate 1/4" jacks. To attach two single-trigger pads—even dual-trigger pads will work as single-trigger pads— you have to use an insert cable. This cable is a stereo plug (tip-ring-sleeve) to two separate mono plugs (see fig. 3.17). The stereo side goes into the drum module and the mono plugs go one each to the individual pads (see fig. 3.18). In my experience, people find this to be the most difficult input to understand. But really, it's quite easy. A dual-mono trigger input is just a way of getting more pad inputs into a smaller space on the drum module. This type of input tends to be found on input types that lend themselves to being mono,

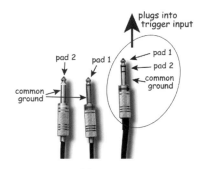

Fig. 3.17

Fig. 3.18

like the kick input. Kick and Tom 3 on the TD-6, and the kick and aux on the TD-8, are all dual-mono trigger inputs. Dual-mono trigger inputs are also found on the HandSonic and SPD-S. There are no dual-mono trigger inputs on Roland's TD-20, TD-12, or TD-10.

> *TIP:*
> *I often use the SPD-S as a sound source to augment my acoustic drums by triggering the kick and snare drum with acoustic drum triggers. This way, not only do I get great snare and kick sounds, I also get the advantage of having nine more pads off to the side of my drums with sound effects, loops, or one-shot samples.*

OK, There Is One More Type of Input

The final type of input is the hi-hat, or foot controller, input. This is where you plug in the hi-hat pedal (Roland FD-6, FD-7, or FD-8) or the control out on the Roland VH-Series hi-hat cymbals. The VH-12 hi-hats are shown here (see fig. 3.19 and fig. 3.20). This input gives you the ability to control the opening and closing of the hi-hats and, on some modules, pitch bend and the ability to vary the number of effects put on a sound. Check your owner's manual to see whether the pedal you're using needs a mono or stereo cable for hookup. Each pedal and module has different requirements.

Fig. 3.19

Fig. 3.20

OK, then. Are you a pad expert now? The information we just covered contains all the big chunks about drum modules and pads. If you have other questions, don't hesitate to call a company's product support line. These guys know it all. Roland has an incredibly knowledgeable product support group.

Trigger Input Response Time: The Faster the Better

Another thing to consider when shopping for a drum module or trigger-to-MIDI interface is trigger response time. This is the amount of time after a pad is hit that sound is heard in the audio outputs (or MIDI information is transmitted via the MIDI out-jack). On all drum modules there is slight delay from when the pad is hit to when the sound comes out of the module. Although small, this amount of delay time is similar to the amount of time that we use to lay back on the beat or to play on top of the beat. Even if a drummer is not developed enough to hear these minor differences in timing, chances are they'll feel that something's not quite right. In the early days of electronic drums, delay times like this were just a fact of life. Today, modern drum modules trigger incredibly fast, to the point where delay times are not perceivable.

> *TIP:*
> *Trigger response time is described in milliseconds. In air, sound moves at about one foot per millisecond (one ms). Roland's TD-20 drum has a trigger response time of less than three milliseconds. This is roughly the time it takes for the sound of your voice, to get to the ear of the person next to you. That's extremely fast!*

The Drum Module and Its Sounds

There are three common ways that sounds show up in drum modules: as PCM sounds (pulse code modulation), sampled sounds, and modeled sounds. Yeah, yeah, you might be saying, "Hey, PCM sounds and sampled sounds are the same thing." Yes, technically they are, but for the sake of our discussion here, they are a bit different—PCM sounds reside in permanent memory (ROM) and sampled sounds reside in erasable memory (RAM) that is emptied when the power is shut off.

PCM Sounds

Again, when I refer to PCM sounds, I'm making the distinction that these sounds are stored in the module's ROM (read-only memory). Although the sounds can be edited by the user, and the edits can be stored and then recalled, the basic sounds themselves can't be deleted from ROM. They are there for good. This is how sounds are stored in most synths, drum modules, and drum machines.

User Sampled Sounds

The sampled sounds I'm referring to are sounds that can be created by the user, stored, and then loaded into a sampler, computer, or sampling percussion pad like the Roland SPD-S. Taking a sound, either acoustic or audio, from something like a CD, and putting it into a form that a sampler can read is called "sampling." These sampled sounds technically are PCM sounds like the ones discussed above, but reside in RAM (random access memory) and can be deleted from memory. They can be saved to the storage memory of a sound module and recalled at will. Currently, the Roland SPD-S is a drummer's premiere sampling drum and percussion product. It has an extremely easy-to-use interface and can store lots of sounds. There is more on the SPD-S Sample Pad in the chapter on sampling.

The beauty of sampling is that you can create, sample, and store your own sounds. These sounds can be your own instruments, "found" sounds such as trash cans and the like, or loops of any kind. We'll cover looping in a later chapter.

Modeled Sounds

Boy, has sound modeling made life easier. Roland has been pioneering modeled sounds for well over a decade. In addition to their V-Drums, modeling technology is found in Roland's guitar synths, VS-Series hard disk recorders, and bass and guitar amps. Let's look briefly at why modeling technology helps make our lives worth living.

One word: Pictures

One Sentence: You can use acoustic drum parameters—head types, shell depth, and even duct tape—to do most of the sound editing!

How Does Modeling Technology Make Life Easier?

Being able to edit sounds and kits using acoustic drum parameters and pictures means we don't have to be technology geeks to create custom drum sets. It's so easy, even a guitar player could do it. Remember, we're using everyday concepts to change the sounds of our acoustic drums to do all the editing on our electronic drums. How forward-thinking is that? Let's look at some screenshots from the groundbreaking Roland TD-20 drum module.

Pick your sound by hitting the drum you want to edit, and the drum module will then note chase to the drum or cymbal you last hit, displaying its information on the screen. Look at the following screenshots taken from the Roland TD-20:

Choose an instrument.

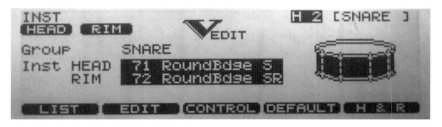

Choose the type of head, and the depth of the drum.

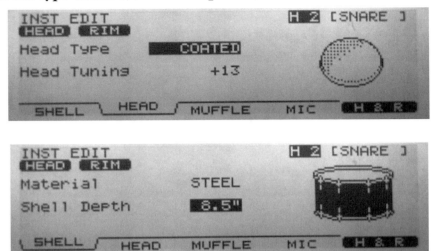

Muffle the drum using duct tape or even a dampening ring.

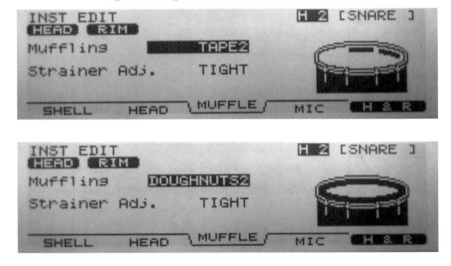

Choose the position of the microphone.

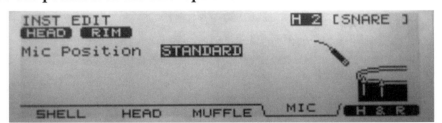

Put rivets or a chain on the cymbals.

You can even choose the type of kick beater you want to use.

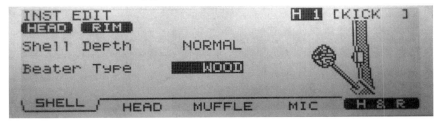

In Conclusion

As you can see, modeling technology makes the learning curve for advanced electronic drums like the TD-20 very easy. I like pictures! Because of this—and the huge advances in pad technology of the last few years—it's no wonder drum electronics is one of the fastest growing parts of drumming.

FOUR

ASSEMBLING YOUR DRUMS FOR THE FIRST TIME

Be it your first electronic drum set or a replacement, congratulations on your new drums! No matter how many kits I've brought home over the years, both acoustic and electronic, it's always an exciting experience. Taking the drums out of the boxes, slipping off the plastic, and setting them up in a way that makes them an extension of the body, can be a religious experience. Adjusting the hardware, tuning the heads, wiping the fingerprints off the shells after setup, and then stepping back to take in the entire picture is incredibly satisfying. Then there's sitting down and playing them. Too much fun!

Most of us look at product instructions, be they written or video, only when we encounter a problem, sort of like a game of "Stump the Chump." Well, I encourage you to break that habit and at least read or look at the drum set's setup instructions. There are subtle setup differences among the various electronic drum sets that will cause you to pull your hair out if you're not aware of them in advance. To help you sidestep some of the common pitfalls, let's look at a few of the most frequent mistakes.

> *Tip:*
> ***Read the instructions enclosed with the drum set.***

Mono & Stereo Cables; Different Lengths

One of the most common problems is using mono cables to plug in pads that need stereo cables to function properly (see fig. 4.1). While some drum sets come with only stereo cables, a few come with a mixture of mono and stereo cables. Stereo cables are for use with the dual-trigger pads, and the mono cables are for use with the single-trigger pads. If you use a mono cable on a dual-trigger pad, the pad's edge sound won't trigger and the choke function will not work.

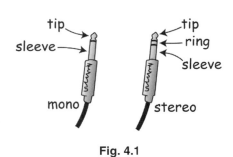

Fig. 4.1

Be aware that the cables used to connect the pads to the sound module may be of varying lengths (see fig. 4.2). Before you haul off and go plugging in cables without advanced planning, unwrap and lay out all the cables before plugging in any of them. Use the shorter cables for the pads closest to the drum module and the longer cables for the pads farthest away. This may seem like an obvious thing to do, but there's nothing more frustrating than trying to plug in the last pad just to find out that cable is too short!

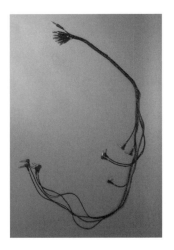

Fig. 4.2

Tom Mounts

This one item alone will make a huge difference on how a drum set feels ergonomically when played, especially drum sets with smaller footprints. The vast majority of electronic drum sets use "L" arm style mounts for the toms. These mounts may have been attached to the stand at the factory, or they may need to be attached as part of the initial setup process. In either case, the "L" arms need to be attached so that they extend out and up (see fig. 4.3). This allows the toms to be positioned farther away from the player, giving a less cramped feel.

Fig. 4.3

A few drum sets, like the Roland V-Compact, come with the mounts and "L" arms already mounted on the stand. Sadly, they're mounted the wrong way. It must be a packaging thing. Don't let this throw you. Take the "L" arm out and stick it in from the other side. You'll be glad you did.

 ## Cymbal Rotation Stoppers

The cymbal rotation stopper is an ingenious little device. As you might suspect, it stops the cymbal from rotating on the cymbal mount (see fig. 4.4). "Why?" you ask. Unlike acoustic cymbals, electronic cymbals have one or two cables plugged into them. If the cymbal is allowed to rotate on the stand like its acoustic brethren, the cables could become increasingly wrapped around the stand. This could result in the cables becoming unplugged, or worse yet, stretched and damaged. Neither of these scenarios is desirable.

Fig. 4.4

Because of the rotation stopper, a cymbal can be tensioned on the stand so it's either floppy (as in the case of a crash), or tight (as in the case of a ride). Even though the cymbal is floppy, it won't rotate on the stand and cause problems with the cables. Yippee!

> *Tip:*
> *Some hi-hat cymbals, like the Roland VH-12, also use rotation stoppers. Make sure you read the directions that come with your hi-hats to see if they use a rotation-stopper assembly of some kind.*

Drum Ergonomics:
Setting Up the Drums to Fit Your Body

As with the discussion of hand technique, there are many differing views on the physical set-up of the drum set. The following are my views and opinions. While they are not the definitive view on drum setup ergonomics, they've served my students and me well for over 35 years. Wow, 35 years! That reminds me, I have a doctor's appointment this afternoon

Whether the drum set has a small footprint, as in the case of the Roland V-Compact TD-3S, or a relatively large footprint like the V-Pro TD-20S, the concept of setup is the same. Your hands and feet should most often be in positions that would be your normal, relaxed position of rest. (That would be daytime, upright rest.)

⠿⠿⠿ Positioning the Feet

Let's find these positions for your feet. The first thing to do is to set a good drum throne (stool) height for your leg length. Adjust the throne height so that your thighs are roughly parallel to the floor (see fig. 4.5). Your calves should be perpendicular to the floor. In my opinion, sitting at either extreme—too high or too low—can interfere with the efficient use of the muscles used to play the pedals.

Fig. 4.5

Fig. 4.6

Next, sit at the throne with your feet positioned in a relaxed, comfortable position. As with every aspect of a good set-up position, it should feel natural (see fig. 4.6). Notice the symmetry between the legs. They are not contorted by an extreme angle either way. This puts the feet in the perfect position to play the pedals. When your feet are in this position, place the pedals there (see fig. 4.7).

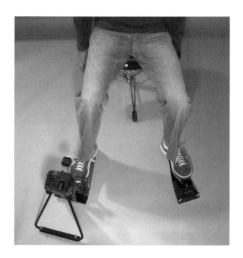

Fig. 4.7

:::::: Placing the Rest of the Drums

As with the pedals, there is a constant theme in placing the remaining parts of the drum set. Everything should be in a place that makes it accessible with a fluid, relaxed, non-contorted motion. I prefer drum setups that are tight and concise. This type of setup will help you get to drums and cymbals quicker, and hit them with better accuracy.

Next, place the drum set rack with the pads off, as shown in fig. 4.8.

Fig. 4.8

To find a good snare drum position, hold a stick in your left hand (right hand if you're going to reverse the drum set for a left-handed player) and bring it into a relaxed playing position (see the chapter on hand technique). Where the tip of the stick falls is where the center of the snare pad should be (see fig. 4.9). Again, there should never be any contortions of body, arms, feet, or legs.

Fig. 4.9

Repeat the process for the remaining tom, hi-hat, and cymbal pads, as shown in the sequence of photos in fig. 4.10.

Fig. 4.10

Getting an Angle on Things

Before you get around to plugging in the pads, you need to make sure that the pads are at an angle that complements the natural, relaxed stick/arm position. Fig. 4.11 shows good set-up angles. Remember, you never want to alter a natural, relaxed hand/arm/stick position to adapt to a drum setup. You want to adjust a drum setup to match a good playing position, not the other way around.

Fig. 4.11

Plugging It All In:
Taming the Spaghetti Monster

Being part of a larger electronic instrument, components must be plugged into a drum module. To date, there's no way of getting around this fact. But I can offer a few tips on wiring up your electronic drum set for the first time so that it looks great and stays tidy.

As stated earlier, the cables used to wire your drum set may be of differing lengths. Use the longer cables to hook up the pads farthest away from the drum module, like the low-tom pads. Use the shorter ones to connect the closest pads, like the hi-hat. It seems a bit simplistic, but it must be said. OK, cabling the drums…

> *TIP:*
> *If you're lucky enough to have a drum set like the Roland V-Pro and V-Stage Series drums, right out of the box they have the necessary cabling run inside the rack directly from the factory. If you wish, you can stop reading this chapter. Go relax and have a beverage!*

Fig. 4.12

Run the cables one at a time, starting with the pad farthest from the drum module and ending with the pad closest to the module. Drape the cords on the inside of the rack, letting the extra cable length hang down near the drum module (see fig. 4.12). All cables will eventually end up being run, and attached along the inside of the drum rack's tubes.

Before doing the final cable clean up, sit down and play the drums to make sure everything is plugged in and working properly. If you attach the cables to the rack without first checking the connections, something invariably will not work correctly. Then you have to tear everything apart and start again. This has put me in grumpy mood more than once.

Making the Drums Look Tidy

Securing the cabling to the rack has more function than just making the drum set look tidy. By taking the time to secure the cables to the rack with wire ties, you'll insure that you won't have to wrestle with the cable monster ever again. You'll be able to break down the drums, fold up the stand, move the drums, and set them back up, all without having to worry about the cables coming loose or becoming tangled.

Here's how I do it…

Begin with the pad farthest from the drum module. Gather the cables and neatly run them along the rack tubes, securing them with wire ties every six inches or so (see fig. 4.13). When you get to the module, bundle up the extra wires, secure them with wire ties, and attach the bundle to the underside of the drum module's mount (see fig. 4.14). You'll end up with a drum set that will stay looking great for years.

Fig. 4.13

Fig. 4.14

FIVE

HAND
TECHNIQUE
Relaxation and Other
Considerations for Electronic Drums

The discussion of hand technique and practice routines is tantamount to wading into a dense quagmire of differing concepts and results. With that in mind, this isn't the definitive discussion of hand technique as it applies to drums, it's just one of many techniques that works. Discussing technique is especially important if your current hand technique isn't relaxed. A relaxed stick grip is essential to maintaining healthy joints, tendons, and muscles in your hands, arms, and shoulders. With a relaxed grip, you'll be able to play longer and faster. This applies directly to acoustic drums as well. In addition to speed and stamina, a relaxed grip tends to get a warmer sound out of an acoustic drum, allowing it to ring longer.

Fig. 5.1

Fig. 5.2

It really doesn't matter whether you play traditional or matched-grip. I play mostly matched-grip (see fig. 5.1). I do this for a number of reasons. First, I play drums (non-pitched) as well as mallets (pitched percussion such as marimba, vibes, etc.). The grip for mallets is based on matched-grip, so I didn't want to increase my practice efforts as I would if I played traditional grip when using drum sticks. Therefore, there was an advantage to playing matched-grip. The second reason was that, at age 16, my understanding of the finer points of traditional grip wasn't very good—frankly, I just didn't understand it back then. So again, matched-grip offered yet another advantage in that I understood it. To this day, about the only time I play traditional grip is when I play brushes, because the brush technique is built around traditional grip (see fig. 5.2). It just feels right. OK, enough about my weaknesses. Let's find some of yours!

If there is one thing you should always remember, it's to be relaxed, *al dente*, Gumby-like. There's a great reason for this. If you are relaxed, you can strike the drum as hard as possible, and you won't injure yourself. There are many stories of drummers injuring themselves by playing drums as hard as they can with a death grip on both sticks. This will work for a while, but eventually you'll seriously hurt yourself. This change to being relaxed may take quite a bit of time. So from now on, constantly monitor the looseness of your stick grip at all times, while practicing and performing. Enough pontificating. Let's get loose.

There's no need for a huge stick when playing electronic drums. So put away the 2S and get out a pair of medium-weight sticks, either wood or nylon tip. I use a stick that is slightly longer than a standard 5A, with an acorn tip, or an electronic stick that I designed for Vic Firth, the eStick (see fig. 5.3). This all-hickory stick has great balance, and is a perfect tip for pads or acoustic drums. Choose a tip you like

Fig. 5.3

while keeping in mind that I've found that a larger tip tends to trigger the pad better than a smaller tip. This might be because of a law of acoustics that says the larger the surface area that sets a membrane in motion (the bigger the tip that hits the pad), the more fundamental mode of vibration is in the resulting waveform (the clearer the trigger spike). Translation: a bigger tip works better. Although sticks can be either wood tip or nylon tip, the eStick comes in wood tip. Choice of stick is based mainly on personal preference, and I prefer that you use mine!

The matched-grip hand position is quite simple and very natural. Without sticks in your hand, let your hands drop naturally to your sides. Now, shake them out so that there isn't any tension anywhere in the shoulders, arms, wrists, or hands. Look at your hands. They more than likely have come to rest so that there is a C-shaped curve to the fingers (see fig. 5.4). This shape is the basis for the matched-grip hand position. The amount of tension in the hands without the sticks is about the same when the sticks are being held. If you're worried about dropping sticks, don't. Just buy another pair or two so that you can grab a replacement quickly.

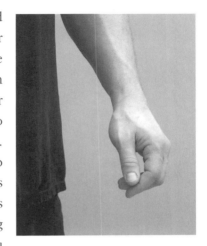

Fig. 5.4

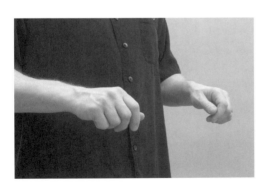

Fig. 5.5

Fig. 5.6

With your arms and hands relaxed at your sides, bend your elbows until your forearm is perpendicular to the floor. The resulting position should come naturally (see fig. 5.5). If there seems to be tension in the hands or wrists, you're trying to put your arms and hands in an unnatural position. People tend to make two common hand-position mistakes. First, they roll the hands over, bend their wrists inward, and put the top of the thumbs pointing up (see fig. 5.6). In this position, the wrists are constricted and don't bend as easily or as far as in the more natural position I describe above (although it's a great timpani grip). Secondly, some people roll their wrists over so that they are flat. In this position, one can feel the increased tension just because of the unnatural hand position

Fig. 5.7

(see fig. 5.7). The other tendency with this position is for the elbows to stick out. The unwanted tension will fight against what you want your hands to do. Remember, you want to be in control of your muscles; you don't want them to be in control of you.

Oh yeah, sticks. Grab one stick and put it in the other hand. The stick is held in the fulcrum (pivot point) created between the first joint of the index finger and the thumb (see fig. 5.8 and fig. 5.9. Further notice that the butt end of the stick comes out about an inch beyond the fleshy part of the hand. The tip of the stick is just an extension of the fulcrum. You should be able to grab the tip of the stick and move it up and down so that it pivots at the fulcrum, without the fingers impeding the motion. The fingers are there not to grip the stick but to guide it, and later to help you play fast. After all, isn't that what we all want to do? (Sorry, that would be guitar players.) OK, repeat with the other hand. If you need a more detailed visual than the photos, go to the *All About Electronic*

Fig. 5.8

Fig. 5.9

Percussion website (http://mikesnyder.net/aaep/) for a video of this motion.

The reason for all the concentration on being relaxed can be traced back to when mesh heads for electronic drums didn't exist. The first sets of electronic drums had very hard surfaces that didn't give at all. It felt a lot like playing a laminate countertop. No, it felt *exactly* like playing a countertop! If you had a death grip on the stick, all the energy from hitting the pad would be transferred into the muscles, tendons, and bones of your hands, wrists, and arms. After playing for any length of time, your hands would hurt and you'd get something akin to tennis elbow, not a good thing. If you had a relaxed grip, most of the energy would travel down the stick and out the end, never to be felt again. Even then, those pads still hurt after a while.

The rubber pads that came next were a big improvement in feel, but they didn't "give" like acoustic drums. So the same was true—you needed a relaxed grip. It wasn't until 1997, with the release of the first generation of V-Drums and the invention of the two-ply mesh head, that we finally got drums that felt great, much like an acoustic drum. Remembering the importance of relaxation, let's now discuss how to play accurately and effortlessly.

With sticks in hand, begin to play a basic warm-up exercise and see how it feels. I prefer the one below—two bars of eighth-note single strokes followed by two bars of sixteenth-note double strokes (see fig. 5.10). This exercise is meant to be simple so you can concentrate on your hand position. Whether you're practicing or playing, you should always be listening to the sound you're producing and monitoring your hand position. The amount of tension in your hands is what you use to produce different sounds from a drum or other percussion instrument. The less tension in your hands, the faster and longer you'll be able to play. Tight hands will limit how fast you can play. If the grip I described is new to you, please play this exercise very slowly, and always practice with a metronome. As with all practice, play the exercise at a tempo that allows you to play from beginning to end without faltering or stopping.

Fig. 5.10

For this exercise, work at a steady tempo for a few minutes, then increase the tempo about five beats per minute (BPM). By increasing the tempo this way, you are working on the exercise as well as strengthening your internal clock by playing at a steady tempo. As with all practice, you should concentrate on relaxation, good hand position, and rhythmic accuracy.

When you play this exercise slowly, you will notice that all the notes, including the double strokes, are played with the wrist only. That is to say, the fingers don't do any of the work. They are relaxed and just follow the motion of the stick, without limiting the travel of the stick in any way. As the tempo of the exercise is increased, there is a range of tempos that can be played with either wrist or fingers. This wrist-to-fingers transition zone (see fig. 5.11) is the most difficult part of the exercise. As your technique gets better, you will find that this area of transition becomes wider, so spend a lot of practice time working on it. Once you are using just your fingers, you are in hyperspace. Even though the tempo is blazingly fast, there isn't a great deal of energy used in hyperspace because you're using fingers. This type of speed and finger control comes gradually. You need to be patient, practice methodically, and use a metronome at all times.

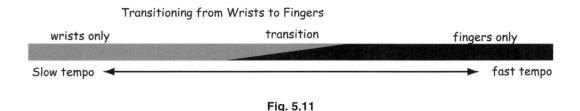

Fig. 5.11

After this exercise becomes more comfortable, move on to other hand exercises you have worked on before, or even completely new exercises, always paying attention to good hand position and relaxation. It is important to spend time working on the rudiments. One place to find them is at the Percussive Arts Society Website (http://pas.org). There are many other sources of additional practice material, both for hand technique and drum set. Teachers, friends, publishers, and the Internet are all great places to begin looking. A bit of advice: don't spend a lot of time practicing things that come easily to you. Spend most of your time working on the material that is the difficult. Practice the hardest things first, leaving the easier material until later in your practice session. At the end, reward yourself with all the fun things—like playing along with recordings and learning new licks.

SIX

AUDIO BASICS AND AMPLIFICATION

Electronic drums and percussion are now in the mainstream. They're tools we use to create and perform music. Because of this, we frequently have to deal with amplifying our electronic instruments, something that only guitar players and keyboard players dealt with in the past. This forces us to learn a new skill set, that of the sound engineer. This is not that difficult—just a few new concepts, some new terminology*, and the ability to listen and learn from other people.

Now that I've scared you, let's move on...

Output Levels, Cables, and Connection Types

There are two basic output levels: line level and mic level. These are the two types of analog output types we'll come across when dealing with electronic and acoustic drums. You might also hear them referred to respectively as balanced and unbalanced, or low-impedance and high-impedance.

*I have to put a bit of a disclaimer here. The standards and terminology I'm going to talk about in this chapter are painted with a wide brush. The audio world isn't as tidy as we all would like it to be; it's a world full of grey areas and near-conformity. There are books written on audio, so if you need to clarify an issue you run into, or a question that arises, hit the bookstore or the Internet and do some searching.

Simply put, line level is a hotter output level than mic level. The majority of electronic drum/percussion sound modules have line-level outputs. In fact, this is the case for almost all synths in general. Line level almost always uses a mono, shielded cable, with a 1/4" plug on both ends to send audio (see fig. 6.1). This cable is a two-conductor cable. The center wire is an insulated, multi-strand wire that is referred to as

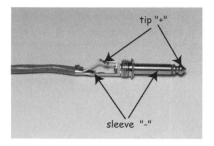

Fig. 6.1

positive (+) and is connected to the tip of the plug. The second conductor, the negative (–) connection, commonly called the shield, is connected to the sleeve or ground of the plug. As the name suggests, the shield wire does just that: it shields the audio signal running through the positive connection from outside radio or magnetic interference. At some point in your life, you've probably heard a radio station come through on a guitar amp or on P.A. speakers. Poor or improper shielding is often the cause of this kind of interference.

TIP:
Buy (or, if you're handy, make) high-quality cables. They last longer and sound better. Many of the cables that I use today I acquired or made in the mid- to late-1980s, all from high-quality cable and connectors.

The line-level, unbalanced connection used on most sound modules is perfect for the typically short cable runs from drum and synth modules to a nearby amplifier. A cable length of about 15 feet is as long as you want to use. After that, you may have problems with signal loss and noise in the audio signal becoming louder in relation to the audio. This is called the signal-to-noise ratio. Remember, hot audio signal—very good. Noise—very bad. If you have to run a

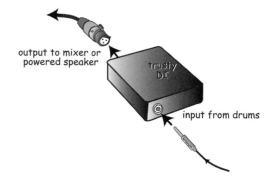

Fig. 6.2

line-level signal over a 15-foot cable length, use a direct box, also known as a DI. A direct box will change the line-level signal to a balanced mic-level signal, which is much more suitable for long cable runs. Fig. 6.2 shows the standard use of a direct box. Keep the 1/4" cable length as short as possible. I carry two passive direct boxes with my drum and percussion electronics. That way, I always have direct boxes available. Better yet, I know they work.

> *TIP:*
> *The direct box has another application: it isolates the ground of the*
> *drum module from the amp or mixing board. If a 60 Hz hum is*
> *heard (a ground loop), there is a "ground lift" switch on the DI, so*
> *flip it the other way and chances are the hum will go away. (Or you*
> *could teach the DI the lyrics.)*

Mic Level

As you just read, a mic-level signal can be run over very long cable lengths with minimal signal loss and minimal increase in the signal-to-noise ratio. For the most part, mic-level signals use XLR connectors. These have three wires: two conductors and a shield (ground). Chances are that you've seen them and touched them. They're called microphone cables (see fig. 6.3).

Fig. 6.3

Amplification and Sound Reinforcement

OK, now that you've got that whole discussion of audio outputs, cables, and connectors committed to permanent memory, let's get on with the task of making our drums sound real LOUD! Remember, it is our collective goal as drummers in the 21st century to get guitar players to tell *us* to turn the volume down. Yes, folks, it's payback time!

Protect Your Hearing

Before we move on, let's talk about hearing protection. Your hearing is very precious and very, very fragile. If you're in loud environments like practice rooms, rehearsal basements, clubs, or concert stages, use hearing protection! For all of my first 25 years of drumming, I never used earplugs. At 36 years of age, I had my hearing checked and fortunately there wasn't too much damage. Mind you, there was some upper mid-range hearing loss in one ear, but rightfully there should have been much more damage, especially after blasting myself with drums in five-by-five practice rooms for countless hours. I've been lucky, but not everyone has.

With that said, get fitted for a pair of musician's earplugs and use them religiously (see fig. 6.4). This style of earplug cuts the sound level relatively equally across the audible frequencies (-15 to -25 db), so the sound you hear is very natural, just quieter. If you don't do this, at least wear a pair of gun muffs when you practice acoustic drums. Not only do they protect your hearing, but they make your acoustic drums sound great!

Fig. 6.4

When it comes to protecting your ears while playing electronic drums, there are a number of things to keep in mind. The pads and cymbals of modern electronic drums make little acoustic sound when they're hit. Obviously, the sound comes from the drum module. So with that in mind you can protect your hearing by being conscious of and limiting the sound output level of the sound module. When practicing or performing with electronic drums, there is no need to match the volume of acoustic drums, which are inherently loud. Whether practicing with an amplifier, P.A., or just headphones, make an effort to keep the audio level as low as possible. You never want to come away from a practice session with your ears ringing. Ringing ears is very bad. I almost never practice with amplification, just a good pair of headphones.

Amplification for Practice, Rehearsal, and Performance

Before we even begin to figure out what kind of amplification or sound reinforcement would be good for specific situations, let's talk headphones. No matter what you plan to do with your electronic drums, no matter what level you are, beginner or professional, buy a good pair of pro-quality headphones. There are many brands, all good. Roland has their top-of-the-line RH-200 headphones (see fig. 6.5), which have great sounding highs and lows and are comfortable on the head. There are also many in-ear or earbud-style headphones out there, like the Shure E2s (see fig. 6.6). Don't use cheap, funky-sounding headphones. Even today's entry-level electronic drums, like the TD-3 based V-Compact, sound incredible. So the better the headphone, the better your experience is going to be.

Fig. 6.5

Fig. 6.6

The type of amplification you need for your electronics is determined by the type of musical situations you'll be in—and by your budget. Budget is not the inhibitor it once was. There are some great, cost-effective options for amplifying drums.

To determine how much of a system you'll need, assess how often you will be involved in the following environments with your electronic drums: practicing, rehearsing, and live performance.

Practice: What Do I Need?

Headphones

The sound requirements for practicing are quite simple. As you just read, all you really need is a good pair of headphones. You can use amplification if you wish, but in my opinion it is overkill, and you lose one of the greatest features of electronic drums, the volume control.

In addition to making sure the headphones have a sound you like and can handle the extreme low and high frequencies that electronic drums have, pick a pair that are comfortable on your head. Keep in mind you'll be wearing these headphones for extended periods, so they must be comfortable. I personally use the Roland headphones and the Shure in-ear monitors.

Stereo, Personal Monitor System

If you really want to use amplification when you practice, Roland makes an amplifier called the PM-3 (see fig. 6.7). This stereo system is not designed to be a stage monitor for performance, but as a personal monitor system for practice and other low-volume situations, like rehearsal. As you can see by the photo, the PM-3 consists of a subwoofer/ amplifier component and two satellite speakers. When set up on the drums, you'll be enveloped in the stereo field so

Fig. 6.7

that when you hit the left crash, it is heard in the left speaker. As you play the toms from high to low, the sound is heard moving across the speakers from left to right (the stereo field) and the subwoofer starts working more as you get to the lower toms and the kick drum, much like what is experienced with acoustic drums.

Rehearsal: What Do I Need?

For me, a band rehearsal is a time to work on music, songs, their form and feel. I try to remember a tune's structure so I can put my cheat sheets away as I become more comfortable with my bandmates' musical side. It's not about playing the music at full-tilt performance volume and energy. In fact, the type of band practice I'm about to talk about, because of the reduced volume, often makes finding a place to rehearse much easier.

Some of the most gratifying rehearsals I've had have been playing my V-Drums. The low volume level of those rehearsals had a lot to do with the enjoyment. If you can keep the guitar player from turning up, you can hear everyone and everything that's going on, and your ears won't ring afterwards.

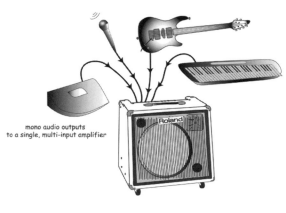

mono audio outputs
to a single, multi-input amplifier

Fig. 6.8

I set up for these rehearsals by using a small P.A., or more often, a multi-channel keyboard amp that everyone can plug into (see fig. 6.8).

I plug the mono 1/4" output of my V-Drums into an open channel—in this case, channel one. This particular amp has stereo inputs, but because there is only one amp, the left and right inputs are mixed together and are heard in mono, so there is no need to plug into it in stereo. Each of the other instruments—in this case, a microphone, guitar, and keyboard—is plugged into the other three channels of the amp. With this setup, each player has separate control over their individual monitor volumes.

TIP:
Don't raise the individual channel volume level higher than the master volume, because this can cause the master output to overdrive and distort.

Live Performance:
How Do I Amplify These Things?

There are three common amplification scenarios:

> 1. Use your own amp or P.A. to monitor and amplify your drums to the audience (front of house).
>
> 2. Use the house P.A. to supply both monitoring and front-of-house sound.
>
> 3. Use the house P.A. for front-of-house sound and use your own monitoring.

A few very general rules of thumb:

> If you're playing a large venue, you have no choice but to use the house P.A.
>
> If you're playing a medium-to-small venue, your personal amplification may be enough, if not for all the sound reinforcement, at least for monitoring yourself onstage.
>
> If you're playing a small room, use your own amplification. It will be more than enough sound amplification and may be the only option, as there probably will not be a house P.A.

There are many different set-up possibilities when one enters the land of live sound reinforcement. I can't cover them all in this book, but I will cover the basics.

Supplying Your Own Amplification

As I just mentioned, if you're playing medium-to-small venues, a small P.A. or an amp designed specifically for drums will probably supply enough sound. As to what a small-to-medium venue is, if a guitar and bass player don't need any amplification beyond their own amps, your own drum amp or small P.A. will probably work. Still, you may want to try out your P.A. setup with your band before taking this recommendation as fact because, as we know, guitar players can play really loud!

Drum Amp

Right now, Roland is the only company making amplifiers designed specifically for drums. The Roland TDA-700 is their top-of-the-line drum amp (see fig. 6.9). It is a great-sounding amp and very loud. A good friend of mine affectionately calls it Big Red. Big Red has three stereo inputs, as well as a stereo link function in which two amps can be used to play in stereo (KC-550 amp, illustrated in fig. 6.8, also has a stereo link function). One of the amps acts as a master mixer, while the other amp is remote. Remember, be sure to use both the left and right master outputs from your drums, not just the mono output. You need to do this so your drums will sound in stereo, the left output in one amp, and the right output in the other.

Fig. 6.9

TIP:
Hook up the left and right outputs so that you hear the sounds of the drums coming from where you'd expect them; i.e., the hi-hat should be heard mostly from the amp on the hi-hat side and the floor tom should be heard mostly from the amp on the floor tom side—just like they would if they were acoustic drums.

Let's look at how to use a drum amp properly...

One Amp: Mono Drums

If only one amp is going to be used, the drums will be in mono. To hook up your drums—with the amp turned all the way down and the electronic drums on—simply take the mono output of the drum module (it's labeled, but is generally the left output) and plug it into a channel on the drum amp. To do this, I use a mono instrument cable. Resist the urge to use that extra stereo cable used to hook up the pads to the drum module because it's not quite designed for sending audio. An instrument cable is shielded to reject interference from radio waves and nearby AC current. NEVER use a speaker cable, since it's not shielded.

TIP:
Don't run audio cables closely parallel to AC cables. This has a tendency to cause hum in the audio signal. If the cables have to cross each other, make them cross perpendicularly.

Next, set the volume control on the electronic drums to about 3/4. This gives you the ability to turn up the drums if a little extra volume is needed later on—you know, to compete with the guitar player getting louder. Next, turn up the amp's master volume knob a little more than half way. Then, while playing the drums (or playing back a sequence of drums), slowly turn up the volume control on the channel that the drums are plugged into until the desired volume level is reached. Simple stuff…

After that, you might want to tweak the EQ on the amp, to tailor the sound of the drums to the room.

> *TIP:*
> *I you want to hear how the drums sound in the audience, have a pre-recorded sequence of one of the beats you play with your band already in your drum's onboard sequencer. That way, the band can play with the sequence and you can go into the audience and listen.*

Using a Small PA: Powered Monitors or Amplifiers

There are a number of great-sounding, small P.A. configurations that are perfect for amplifying electronic drums.

Configuration One

Powered monitors, with at least a 15" woofer and a horn, are big enough to handle the extreme low and high frequencies that drums have. These speakers have power amps built into them, so they don't need separate ones. That means fewer things to lug around. As with the drum amps, you'll need one speaker if you want to play in mono and two if you want to play in stereo

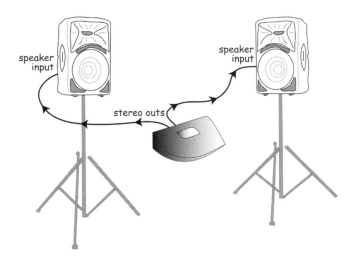

Fig. 6.10

(see fig. 6.10). To me, playing in stereo is always more gratifying.

There are a couple of ways to plug your drums into these powered speakers, although it's not quite as easy as it is with the drum amp.

As a rule, powered speakers use XLR-type inputs. These are the types of cables microphones use. If the powered speakers you're using have XLR, balanced-type inputs, you'll have to use one of these two ways to get the unbalanced outputs from your drums into the XLR inputs:

1. Use a specially-wired cable, XLR to mono 1/4. You can purchase this cable or, if you're good with a soldering iron, make one from a microphone cable. Pin one (ground) and pin three from the XLR are soldered to the sleeve (ground) of the 1/4" jack. Pin 2 of the XLR is soldered to tip of the 1/4" jack. This cable is readily available at any music store. While this is one solution, if you get a ground loop (60-cycle hum) between the electronic drums and the speakers, the next method solves this problem.

2. A better solution is to use direct boxes. As an electronic drummer, they're something you should have in your bag of tricks. This particular direct box has been in my electronic box since the late 1980s (see fig. 6.11).

Fig. 6.11

When using direct boxes to plug in your electronic drums, use the following cable routing:

Plug a short 1/4" instrument cable into the outputs of your electronic drums, then plug the other end of that cable into the input of the direct box. Then, using a microphone cable, connect the XLR output of the direct box to the input of the speaker. Look back at fig. 6.2 if you want to review the routing illustration. If you're running in stereo, do this for both the left and right outputs. You'll need two direct boxes for two speakers.

Configuration 2

This method uses a small mixing board in conjunction with the power monitor(s). It offers a great deal of flexibility (see fig. 6.12).

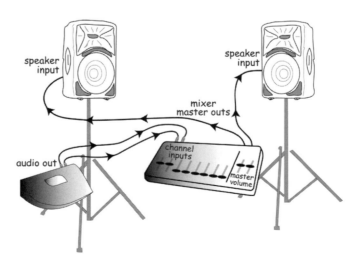

Fig. 6.12

Configuration 3

This procedure is similar to the previous speaker set-up, but replaces the mixer and the powered speakers with two (or one, if mono) keyboard amps, like Roland's KC-550s or KC-350s (see fig. 6.13). These amps function not only as

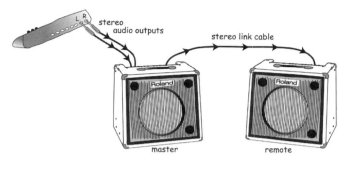

Fig. 6.13

powered speakers, but also have a mixer built right into them, which eliminates the need for a separate mixer. One less piece of gear to move around is always good in my book.

Configuration 4

Now, if you really don't mind moving gear, add a sub-woofer to the previous set-up for the best-sounding, most flexible (yet compact) drum P.A. you can get (see fig. 6.14). You get the smoothness of the KC-350s (slightly smaller that the KC-550s), and the low-end thump and rumble of the subwoofer. This is my favorite set-up!

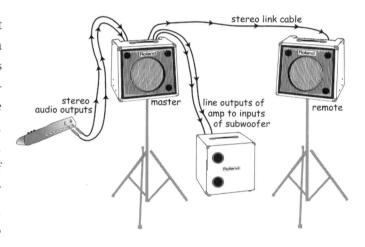

Fig. 6.14

Using House Sound

Provided the house sound system is a good-sounding one, this option is great because you don't have to move gear. The down side is that you are at the mercy of both the sound engineer and the quality of the sound system. Could be good or could be bad. The bit of wisdom I'd pass on here is to be as flexible and as nice to the sound crew as you can. They can make you sound as good or as bad as they want.

This situation would be one to break out your DIs and offer them for use on your drums. There frequently seems to be a shortage of direct boxes. With your DIs, also pack a few extra short 1/4" patch cables. The cables to get from the drum module to the DIs are the player's responsibility.

Using House Sound and Your Own Monitoring

There's not much difference here from using the house sound system, except that you'll need to split the output signal from the drum module so that there are duplicate outputs, whether stereo or mono. These will connect to the amplifier or powered speakers you're using for monitoring. Depending on the drum module you have, here are three common ways of doing just that:

1. Most DIs have a parallel output, which means you can split off a 1/4" output directly from the DI itself, no special tricks needed, just an extra cable or two (see fig. 6.15). The input from your drums will be sent to the house P.A. Take the 1/4" output and plug it into your amp or PA. Remember, you'll need two sets of cables and two DIs when you run sound out in stereo.

Fig. 6.15

2. Fig. 6.16 shows a routing that is possible if you have an amplifier that has direct outputs. These outputs take the place of the direct boxes. Take the audio outputs from your drums and plug them into your amp, like the Roland TDA-700 and KC-Series amplifiers. Plug your drums into the audio

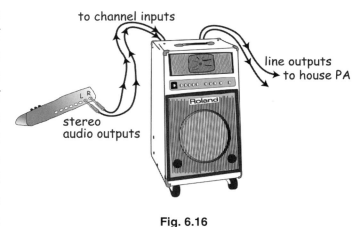

Fig. 6.16

inputs of the amp, then have the sound crew plug the line outputs on your amp into the house sound system.

Although the amp line outputs take the place of the DIs, they don't always offer the protection against ground loops. I've been in situations where I've had to use DIs to get rid of ground hum issues. Redundant, but effective.

3. Some of the newer drum modules, like the Roland TD-20, have the option of duplicating the master outputs as part of the mixer/output assignments. In this situation, take one set of outputs (mono or stereo) to your monitors and the duplicate set to the house system.

In Conclusion

This chapter should give you a good start on understanding and dealing with audio in "the real world." Keep you eyes and ears open and learn from those around you; your peers are a huge source of information. Your experiences, both mistakes and successes, will also be a source of learning.

SEVEN

BASIC MIDI

"We're not in Kansas anymore."

Unless you're going to sequence to a computer or trigger the sounds of an external sound source, most of today's electronic drums are designed so you don't need to understand the inner  workings of MIDI. But it's still there beneath the surface, diligently doing its thing while you're playing. Roland's entire line of electronic drums are plug-and-play—no muss, no fuss—just like the Apple Macintosh on which I'm writing this book. Out of the box, the gear works easily and doesn't get in the way of creating music and having fun. After all, that's why we got into music in the first place, isn't it?

So, if you fall into the pile of humanity that just wants to play and perform with your electronic drums, you could stop reading this chapter now, set up your drums, plug in an amp or set of headphones, and wander off into the wonders of electronic drums! Of course, I strongly suggest that you read through this chapter at least once, in the hopes that some of the information sticks in your subconscious. Invariably, the newbie to electronic drums will soon discover the power and flexibility they have in their hands, then it's off to MIDI-land at lightning speed. So, best get a head start now. Over the years, I've seen it happen a million times. OK, not quite a million, but definitely more than two. Point being, MIDI will eventually become a friend and occasionally an enemy. There's no getting around it.

What Is MIDI?

The concept of MIDI can seem a bit abstract at first exposure. After all, up until now the most difficult decision we drummers had to make was generally, "birch or maple" and "wood or plastic tip?" We've had to perish the thought of actually plugging in a cable! So, resist the urge to turn and flee. I'll make the basics of MIDI as easy as possible.

MIDI is an acronym for Musical Instrument Digital Interface. MIDI isn't something physical you can touch. It is a common communication language that most modern electronic musical instruments and computers use to "talk" to one another, even though they may be from different manufacturers. MIDI does not transmit audio— it sends event information that represents your performance. This information is sent in the form of a MIDI message. There are different kinds of information that can be sent via MIDI, including MIDI channel, note number, note on, note off, velocity, and patch change. There are other types of MIDI information too, some even used exclusively for drums and percussion.

MIDI: The Beginnings

Before MIDI was conceived, polished, and adopted by the music manufacturers, it was difficult to connect two or more synthesizers from the same manufacturer together, let alone those from two or more different manufacturers. I can remember more than a few keyboard players loudly cursing the synthesizer companies with words I can't repeat here. Players desperately needed an easier way to interface keyboards. Fortunately, there were people in the musical instrument manufacturing industry who felt the same way, and what they came up with was revolutionary. It changed the face of music.

In the early 1980s, Ikutaro Kakehashi, founder of Roland Musical Instruments, and Dave Smith of Sequential Circuits spearheaded MIDI's initial development. Perhaps more importantly, they created an atmosphere in which the various manufacturers could have an open dialogue regarding this new, universal communication language. They both saw a need for a common communication protocol for electronic musical instruments. Their work prompted other American and Japanese companies to discuss this common need, ultimately culminating in the release of MIDI Specification 1.0 in 1983. Although the MIDI spec is often called slow and outdated, it continues to serve the needs of musicians over two decades later. It is virtually unchanged from its original 1983 specifications, a testament to its completeness at first inception. Some type of MIDI-enabled gear is used on almost all the music we hear, regardless of genre.

The first instruments on the market to utilize this new standard were the JX-3P from Roland and the Prophet 600 from Sequential Circuits. Although these instruments were greeted with much success and acclaim, it was another instrument, Yamaha's DX-7, that captured the buying public's interest, reportedly selling in the neighborhood of nearly 200,000 units over its lifetime. It had a new sound, that of FM synthesis. It was relatively light and easy to use, unless of course you were trying to program new sounds on it—not easy on a good day. These new instruments replaced the heavy and bulky Fender Rhodes that keyboard players had been lugging to gigs for years. Finally, the chains of bondage had been broken. There was no longer a need to haul heavy keyboard gear or play funky, out-of-tune acoustic pianos that couldn't be heard over the din of wailing guitars anyway. Life was better.

These instruments also made possible the new area of computer- and hardware-based MIDI sequencing. Sequencing is the recording of performance data without actually recording the performance's audio. The performance data recorded, in its most basic form, is what note was played (note number and MIDI channel), how loud the note was played (velocity), and at what point in time it was played.

MIDI has continued to grow in a few ways since 1983, making it possible to save MIDI data in a universal format called the Standard MIDI File (SMF). Not only would a MIDI sequence be able to be saved so that it could be opened up with another manufacturer's software or hardware sequencer, but it would play back with all the nuance and accuracy of the original performance.

There was also agreement among the manufacturers to create a standardized MIDI sound set, called the General MIDI standard (GM). With this sound set, an SMF always knows how to find the sounds it needs.

If you'd like to know a bit more about the history of MIDI, do an Internet search. It's rather amazing that the entire musical instrument industry got together and made this communication protocol work. Because of their cooperation, we're all winners. Thanks to Mr. Ikutaro Kakehashi, Mr. Dave Smith, and their respective staffs for this great contribution to the world of music.

At the time of this writing, there are a few changes taking place in the way MIDI is transferred. There are now a number of instruments using ISO 1394, commonly called Firewire, to transfer MIDI data between instruments. In addition to MIDI, Firewire can carry eight or more tracks of digital audio between devices. The use of Firewire simplifies cord patching and makes setups simpler and more stable. Look for continuing changes in how MIDI is delivered.

Things You Can Do with MIDI

Most of the initial time spent with a new electronic drum set will be putting it through its paces, playing the different kits (patches), and generally having fun. There will be untold hours lost chopping wood, working out your cool licks, and just having a great time playing the drums. The electronic drum experience definitely brings back the reason we all started playing in the first place—fun! I guarantee, though, that there will come a time that you'll want (or be pushed) to explore what MIDI can do to expand the capabilities of your drum set. It can do so in a number of ways:

Record to an External Sequencer (which may include digital audio capabilities)

You can record to an external MIDI sequencer, like a computer with the appropriate software, or to a keyboard workstation. Your performance can be manipulated after the fact. That is, timings of individual hits, as well as the sounds of the different drum instruments, can easily be changed at any time.

Sequence to a Drum Set's Onboard Sequencer*

Record your playing and analyze it while practicing. Create loops quickly and easily.

Trigger an External Sound Module from Your Drums

In this situation, you can play the sounds of another sound module just by plugging in one MIDI cable between them. You hit your drums, and you hear the sounds of the external module.**

Have an External Controller Play Your Drum Module

If you have an external controller, like a Roland SPD-Series Percussion Pad, or a compact keyboard controller, like an Edirol PCR-M1, you can plug it into your drum module with a single MIDI cord. The controller will be able to play your drum module, even while you're playing the drums with the pads.

*Found on most intermediate and high-end drum sets.
**OK, I'll admit that there are a few settings that need to be changed if you want to play non-drum sounds, but if you want to trigger drum and percussion sounds from the external sound module, plug and play should work. The General MIDI specification makes this so.

The above uses of MIDI are just a few of the most basic scenarios. An entire book could be dedicated to the many ways you can apply MIDI to real-life situations. In addition to reading and experimenting, I suggest that you befriend a MIDI guru in your area. Augment your learning by watching and listening to them. They don't even have to be a drummer because MIDI is MIDI, no matter what the instrument.

Let's Talk Basic MIDI ...
Like, "MIDI is not audio."

Please keep in mind that MIDI is not audio, so when you record MIDI you're not recording audio like you would with tape or hard-disk recorders. When MIDI is recorded, it records only performance data: which drum or cymbal was hit, when it was hit, how hard it was hit, etc. Unlike audio, this data can easily be altered after the performance. Timings can be changed, volumes can be altered, and notes can even be added or deleted.

The basic way MIDI moves information between instruments is relatively simple. Here's a brief explanation of what happens when you play a note on an electronic drum:

1. When the drum is hit, the pad sends a trigger signal to the drum module.

2. The drum module recognizes the trigger signal.

3. The drum module then sends a note-on MIDI message via the MIDI-out port including, at minimum, the following information:

   a. The MIDI channel to which the pad is assigned (1-16, defaults to 10 for drums).

   b. The note number assigned to the pad.

   c. Velocity data showing how hard the pad was hit (volume).

   d. A note-off command may also be sent to tell the drum module to stop playing. Within the MIDI specification, it is allowable not to send a note-off command for non-pitched drums and percussion. Drum and percussion sounds are of a fixed length and stop sounding on their own. This cuts down on the density of the MIDI data stream.

The MIDI data sent is a numeric representation of a performance, frequently referred to as performance data. Clever, huh? Thank you, Mr. Kakehashi and Mr. Smith. This basic message embodies the simplistic beauty of MIDI. Again, the data described above captures a player's performance, without recording the audio of that performance, leaving open the ability to capture, edit, and change the sounds of a performance at a later time. As you'll see in the chapter on sequencing, working this way can give you incredible flexibility throughout every step of creating and performing music. I often use this technology at home to work remotely on projects in locations all over the world.

The basic MIDI message described above is the same for every MIDI-capable instrument, be it a keyboard, guitar, drums, or hand-percussion controller. (I absolutely love my HandSonic.) That is to say, the basic MIDI message that is needed to make a sound module play is almost the same for every MIDI instrument. When I use the words instrument, keyboard, or drums, I'm inferring that it is a MIDI instrument. Again, the basic message consists of—at least—MIDI channel, note number, note-on, velocity, and perhaps even a note-off command. Every time a drum pad is struck, provided it's plugged into a drum sound module or other trigger-to-MIDI interface, this basic message is sent out via the MIDI-out port. The external sound module receives and responds to the information that was sent from the MIDI-out port. This simple message opens up a whole new world of sound, performance, and recording possibilities. Right now, let's look at some basic MIDI parameters and their functions.

Let's Talk Basic MIDI Parameters

Note Numbers

There are 128 different note numbers. Note number information is found in the note-on and note-off part of the MIDI message. Numbers are assigned to the chromatic notes of the keyboard. This is done sequentially, from low to high, with Middle C most often being note number 60. You might be saying, "OK, I don't play keys, I play drums! How are notes assigned to drums?" Well, it's back to the MIDI specification for that information. The General MIDI specification spells out in detail what drum sounds are assigned to what note numbers. Depending on drum set configuration, some of the notes assignments might vary a bit, but the main drums like the snare drum and kick drum will always be the same.

Out of the box, the notes assignments for Roland V-Drums are as follows (TD-20*
used here, as it has the most note assignments of the Roland drum modules):

Kick	#36
Kick Rim	#35
Snare	#38
Snare Rim	#40
Tom 1	#48
Tom 1 Rim	#50
Tom 2	#45
Tom 12 Rim	#47
Tom 3	#43
Tom 3 Rim	#58
Tom 4	#41
Tom 4 Rim	#39
Hi-Hat Bow, Open	#46
Hi-Hat Bow, Closed	#42
Hi-Hat Edge, Open	#26
Hi-Hat Edge, Closed	#22
Hi-Hat w/Foot	#44
Crash 1 Bow	#49
Crash 1 Edge	#55
Crash 2 Bow	#57
Crash 2 Edge	#52
Ride Bow	#51
Ride Bell	#53
Ride Edge	#59

*The TD-20's MIDI note assignments are an extension of the GM specification, as drum technology
has grown much faster than the specification.

> *TIP:*
> *Almost all MIDI data is represented by values between 0-127, or sometimes 1-128 (128 steps in either case). There are 128 note numbers and 128 levels of velocity, volume, and continuous controller data like hi-hat open-to-closed, to name just a few. Why the number 128 is used will become clearer under the discussion "Bits and Bytes" later in this chapter.*

MIDI Channels

There are 16 MIDI channels. (Yes, I know… not a value of 128. This is one of the few exceptions.) The way MIDI channels work is quite ingenious. Every sound module can be set to receive exclusively on at least one MIDI channel. The General MIDI specification dictates the channels to be used for each group of instruments: piano, bass, drums, etc., with drums by default being set to MIDI Channel 10. Sound modules will respond only to MIDI data on MIDI channels they're set up to receive. For instance, a drum module set up to receive on MIDI Channel 10 will ignore all note-on data it receives on any other MIDI channel. In fact, it will ignore *all* MIDI data until it sees data on MIDI Channel 10. Then it will spring to life and dutifully process that data without question.

Connecting Together Multiple Sound Modules

A MIDI instrument receives and transmits MIDI data via the MIDI-in and MIDI-out ports. As I just mentioned, an instrument, depending on its design, can be set to transmit and receive data on one or more MIDI channels (a sound module that can receive on more than one MIDI channel is called multi-timbral). As you can see in fig. 7.1, there can be multiple external MIDI instruments connected together using MIDI. One just daisy-chains the MIDI-out of the first one to the MIDI-in of the next device, then continues chaining the MIDI-thru of that device to MIDI-in of yet the next device, and so on to any subsequent devices.* As drummers, we won't find the need to use this daisy-chain routing very often, because we usually employ only one external sound module.

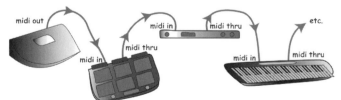

Fig. 7.1

*Although daisy-chaining works, it is not the best way to hook together multiple MIDI instruments, because there is a lag time introduced into the MIDI data stream each time it passes through a device. If there are more than a few devices chained together in this fashion, the lag time or MIDI delay becomes quite noticeable. There is MIDI hardware designed to eliminate this problem, as well as interfaces that can connect all of your MIDI devices to your computer.

Drum-Specific and Other Types of MIDI Data

Continuous controller is another type of MIDI data that is very important for electronic drums. Continuous controller data (cc for short) allows you to affect one or more notes in real time. That is to say, a sound can be changed by continuous controller information in various ways as it is sounding. Continuous controller data is used almost constantly when playing most of today's electronic drums, because it is used to make the hi-hat move smoothly from open to closed. You'll also see this data quite a bit when sequencing drums on the computer. As you've probably already guessed, cc data has 128 different values (0–127).

In Electronic-drum Land, we regularly see these seven different continuous controllers used (even though there are many more):

Modulation (#1)

Foot Controller (#4)   Hi-Hat, Open (127), to Closed (0)

Volume (#7)   Volume, None (0), to Full Volume (127)

General Data Slider (#16)   Positional Sensing

General Data Slider (#17)   Positional Sensing

General Data Slider (#18)   Positional Sensing

Controller (#100 & #101)   Pitch Bend via Hi-Hat Pedal

Of the seven controllers listed above, Foot Controller (#4) is the most used of all. Since 1992, with the debut of the world's first complete electronic drum set, the Roland TDE-7K, Continuous Controller #4 has been used to gradually open and close the hi-hat. This has become the *de facto* standard in the electronic drum world. As an aside, this hi-hat function, along with the chokeable cymbals also found on this drum set, was a huge improvement that Roland pioneered. These two new functions allowed us drummers to have a complete electronic drum set for the first time ever.

In the case of the hi-hat, MIDI controller information is working for you without you even knowing it. Fig. 7.2 shows the hi-hat MIDI information recorded by sequencing software. In addition to the hi-hat continuous controller data, you'll also see note-on information and timing data displayed as to where the note falls in the measure. The information you see here, displayed as

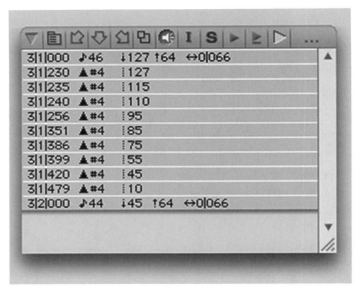

Fig. 7.2

event data, was recorded in Mark of the Unicorn's Digital Performer software. For the sake of this demonstration, I've recorded one open hi-hat note on the downbeat of measure three, and gradually shut the hi-hat until it was completely closed on the downbeat of beat two. You'll notice that the open hi-hat is Note Number 46, and the closed hi-hat note is Note Number 44, and the continuous controller hi-hat data goes from 127 (open) to 10 (near closed).

Getting MIDI From Here to There

The MIDI protocol makes it easy to set up communication between two or more devices. Every MIDI-capable device, such as a drum sound module, will have one or more of these MIDI ports: in, out, thru, or out/thru. These devices are connected to one another with a MIDI cable. The two ends of this cable are identical, each terminating in a 5-pin din plug (see fig. 7.3).

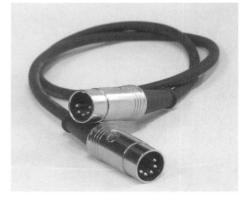

Fig. 7.3

Before we dive into the nuts and bolts of MIDI protocol, let's look at a few basic MIDI configurations. That's just a fancy way of saying "Let's plug MIDI cords into our setup so that MIDI messages move correctly from instrument to instrument, instrument to computer, etc."

The Most Common Drum MIDI Configuration

To play the sounds of an external sound source (like a Roland SPD-S sample pad) from your electronic drums, simply plug the MIDI-out of your drum module into the MIDI-in of the external sound source. That's it—just one MIDI cable. With this configuration, your drums can communicate with the external sound module, but that external module can't talk to your drums (see fig. 7.4). Your drums are the controller for the external sound source. In my experience, this is the most common live-performance MIDI setup used for drums. Remember, MIDI-out to MIDI-in.

Other settings are needed to make the sound modules communicate properly, the most important being that the external sound module is set to receive on the same MIDI channel that your drums are transmitting. Your drums will be set at the factory to transmit (and receive) on MIDI Channel 10. If you're triggering another external drum or percussion sound module (like a Roland SPD-20 or SPD-S), the channels are preconfigured for this setup to work properly.

The beauty of this setup is that by hitting just one pad you can play sounds from both the drum module and the external sound module at the same time. This is called layering sounds. These can be similar sounds, like two complementary snare drums, or vastly different sounds like a snare drum and a tambourine. When a MIDI cord gets involved, a vast new sound palette is opened up. Use your imagination.

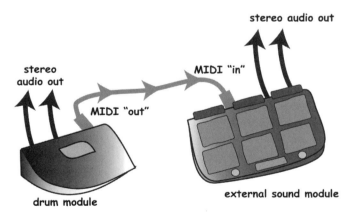

Fig. 7.4

Bits and Bytes... For the Brave

Here's where you learn a little about how MIDI works at the binary level. You remember what binary code is, don't you? All microprocessor-based devices, including your microwave, MP3 player, calculator, and your electronic drums use binary code. Is it coming back to you yet? No? OK. To refresh quickly, a byte is made up of eight bits, represented by ones and zeros, high and low, on and off. Fig. 7.5 shows how two bytes might look above the voltage of the actual MIDI signal as recorded by an oscilloscope. Anything that contains microchips uses bits and bytes. The power switch is either on or off, high or low. Nowadays it's hard to find anything that doesn't contain some kind of microchip and, therefore, the binary code that makes it work. My toothbrush even has a microchip.

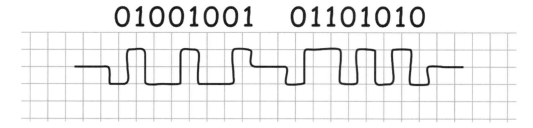

Fig. 7.5

Inside the Basic MIDI Message

Although the MIDI information generated by an instrument is generally more complex than what follows, the MIDI data below shows the minimum information needed to play an external instrument. It is also the exact same information that a sequencer records to capture a MIDI performance accurately. I have to point out here that you will never see the MIDI data in the actual bits and bytes I am about to speak of. It is presented here as just a little insight into the inner workings of MIDI data.

The basic MIDI message consists of a minimum of three bytes of information: Status Byte, Data Byte 1, and Data Byte 2. These three bytes make up what is called the channel voice message. Here's what this channel voice message looks like in more detail:

Status Byte (Byte 1)

1001cccc

> The status byte contains two snippets of information: the type of information to be contained in the following data byte(s), and the MIDI channel on which this data is being transmitted. The first half of the byte, 1001 in this case, is the type of status byte. (Here, it denotes that the data bytes to follow are note-on information). The second half of the byte, represented here by cccc, is the MIDI channel transmit number, a value from 1-16. Why only 16 values? This is because the four digits that make up the second half of this byte can be arranged into no more than 16 unique combinations (2^4); 0000, 0001, 0011, 0111, etc.

Data Byte (Byte 2)

0nnnnnnn

> Where nnnnnnn is the note number value, 0-127 (128 different values). Look out, more math! The seven digits, nnnnnnn, can be arranged into 128 unique combinations (2^7). How tidy is that?

Data Byte (Byte 3)

0vvvvvvv

> Where vvvvvvv is the note on velocity value, 0-127 (127 values, velocity 0=note off). As above, there are seven digits, (2^7), 128 unique combinations. In musical terms, we think of velocity as volume. But, as you'll discover later, in MIDI-land, volume is yet another MIDI control parameter.

That wasn't so bad was it? This bits-and-bytes arrangement is used in every computer. It is the byte that dictates that almost every value in Computerland is a multiple or division of 256. A byte can represent 256 different and distinct numeric values. 2^8. There you go, quick primer on bits and bytes for those of you who missed class that day. Now, for the time being, my sadistic desires are satiated.

MIDI Wrap

This is just a primer on what MIDI is, and what can be done with it. More will be covered in the next chapter, "Basic MIDI Sequencing." Even with all the information on MIDI presented in this book, I've only scratched the surface of what can be done. Continue reading, asking questions, searching, making mistakes, and asking more questions. MIDI-land is a vast world. Explore it.

EIGHT

BASIC MIDI
SEQUENCING

Where My MIDI Adventure Began

I first began my venture into Computerland on a Macintosh in March 1984. At that time, and into the early '90s, the Mac was the platform of choice for any type of creative use. There was quite a difference between Macs and PCs of that era. PCs couldn't even come close to doing the job of a Macintosh. It just couldn't happen. That being said, the last ten years have brought about major changes in computer operating systems, hardware, and software. These changes have almost brought down the Mac/PC Tower of Babel, making the choice of computer platform one of personal preference, not necessity. As I sit here at my desk writing, there are both Macintoshes and PCs in my studio. OK, the PC in my studio still makes me feel like a traitor, but my therapist and I are working hard on getting me through this. Enough about me…

Sequencing: Putting Things in the Right Order

I know some of you are still recovering from the last chapter on MIDI, so if you need to take a break, go do it. Have a beverage, walk the dog, or wash the car. Tackle this chapter when you're refreshed. This is the where we begin to get into the practical application of what's already been covered in the previous chapters. For me, this is always the fun part of learning. This—and recess. The foundation presented here will follow you throughout your entire music career, regardless of the type of performing or recording you're involved in.

Sequencing: Let's Define It

Sequencing describes one of the chief tools used in modern music production (that and the coffee grinder). Quite simply, sequencing is the act of putting things in a desired order. In music production, the things we put in order are MIDI data and sometimes digital audio. The desired order is the one that makes sense to us—or the person signing the check. We put data in order using a sequencer, which is a stand-alone hardware device or software program for a computer that records, edits, and stores this ordered data. The ordered data (the all-knowing author writes with pompous reiteration) is the MIDI performance data representing our drum performance. I'm sure you remember from the last chapter: our performance is what drum is hit, how hard it is hit, and when it is hit.

What Gear Do I Use to Sequence My Performance?

There two basic types of devices currently used to capture or sequence a MIDI performance. They are the keyboard workstation, and sequencing software running on a computer, be it an Apple Macintosh or a Windows PC. Although you'll probably gravitate to one of these three devices, truth be told, you need a basic understanding of all the hardware and software available. Specifics of operation are why there are manuals with indexes. Once you learn the common terminology of sequencing and music electronics in general, use the index to quickly find the information you need. The indexes of most electronics and software manuals written today are quite extensive. Make them your friends.

Choosing a Primary Sequencing Platform (Please, tell me what gear to use!)

Again, you have two sequencer platform choices to pick from, a keyboard workstation, or a computer (Macintosh or PC) and sequencing software. There are many choices out there, so test-drive a few before choosing. This is a good time to ask friends and other people in the know for recommendations. I prefer to use a Macintosh most of the time, but the choice of what platform (hardware) you use to sequence MIDI isn't that crucial because you can't really make a wrong choice. One of the great things about working only with MIDI (with no digital audio involved) is that you can use almost any type of sequencing platform. You simply have to be able to deliver the finished sequences on media that the other person can read (floppy, CD-ROM, email, etc.). The choice of platform becomes much more crucial, however, when you begin to put digital audio together with MIDI data. But we'll get to that in a later chapter. In fact, MIDI data transfers quite easily between any device that records MIDI data. This is because the MIDI spec allows a MIDI sequence to be saved in the Standard MIDI File (or SMF) format, which can be read by every modern hardware and software sequencer available. (SMF file names all end with ".mid.") If you're using a workstation, you're able to output SMFs either to floppy disk, removable media like Compact Flash, or directly to the computer itself via USB. Every sequencer will read Standard MIDI files. (OK, if you find one that doesn't, just keep it to yourself. I'm not only prone to broad statements, but easily provoked to violence as well).

While I have one primary application I use to sequence (and record digital audio), there are a number of other applications that I use less frequently, in order to be more compatible with certain clients.

Local Control, Clicks, Ticks, and Quantizing

A discussion of the mystic setting on your drum module called Local Control has to take place before we get on with our jump into the world of sequencing. You're probably saying to yourself, "Local, huh?" If you are, have faith and read on. It will be revealed, Grasshopper.

You'll find this setting somewhere amongst the global MIDI settings of your drum module. The word "global" is used to describe settings or parameters that affect the entire sound module, regardless of the patch (kit) being used. Local Control is one of those global settings. Every controller with sounds onboard has this setting. Local Control on a drum module will generally have a factory default setting of "On."

Local Control: On

Don't freak. The concept of Local Control is quite simple. When Local Control is on, the drum module will make a sound when you hit a pad. The way a drum module comes out of the box is with Local Control on; that is, the drum module is being controlled "locally" by the pads. This is the way your drum module will be set most of the time for practicing and performing.

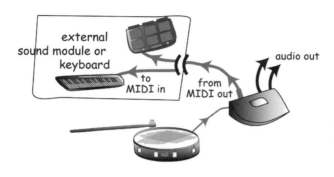

Fig. 8.1

With Local Control on, the chain of events is as follows. You hit the pad and the assigned sound exits the audio outputs at the same time the corresponding MIDI information is sent out the MIDI-out of the drum module (see fig. 8.1). This is the configuration used to trigger external sound modules like a Roland SPD-S sample pad or a keyboard using MIDI. Looking at fig. 8.1, notice that there is only one MIDI cable being used. It is connected from the MIDI-out of the drum module to the MIDI-in of the external device (sound module, keyboard workstation, or computer). Follow along with fig. 8.1. Again, the pad is hit. In reaction to this hit, audio is sent to the audio outputs, and at the same time MIDI information assigned to the pad is sent out the MIDI-out jack. This is the common set-up for live performance

Local Control: Off

Conversely, Local Control off is just that: the pads do not directly make the drum module produce audio. The MIDI is sent to the sequencer, then patched through to the sequencer's MIDI-out (computer or workstation). It's the MIDI information received by the drum module from the computer that produces the sound.

Let me say this a second way. This is the order of events with Local Control off: the pad is hit, the drum module doesn't send audio to the audio outputs because of the hit, but it does send the assigned MIDI information for the pad to the sequencer via the MIDI output. That MIDI data is recorded into the sequencer, then passed back out (run through) the MIDI-out of the computer and is received by the MIDI-in of the drum module. The drum module doesn't make a sound (doesn't send its audio to its audio outputs) until the MIDI data coming back into the drum module plays the assigned sound.

To put it yet a third way, hitting the pad sends the MIDI information to the sequencer, but doesn't make the drum module send out audio. The MIDI data that's patched through to the drum module's MIDI-in is what makes the drum module send out the audio.

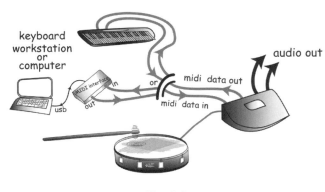

Fig. 8.2

If you're scratching your head, check out the next diagram and follow the routing as you reread these paragraphs (see fig. 8.2). This is the most common setup used when sequencing. Understanding the concepts of "Local Control on/off" and "patch though" are essential to understanding more complex MIDI setups and routing. So, make sure you understand them! You'll also notice the addition of a MIDI interface between the drum module and the computer. This interface translates the MIDI data into a format the computer can read. These days it most often is USB.

> *TIP:*
> *After sequencing with Local Control "Off" be sure to set it back to "On". Otherwise, the next time you use your drums you may find yourself pulling your hair out trying to figure out why they aren't making any sound. (This has never happened to me, of course!)*

The Dreaded Click Track

There is no rule that dictates the order in which instruments are to be sequenced or recorded. You might be inputting drums to a click track without any other instruments, or you could be sequencing the drums after every other part is recorded. Be ready for anything. One thing is for sure—you will be working with a click of some sort. That's why you should always practice with a metronome. It develops a steady inner clock and helps make playing to a click or loop much less nerve-racking when you're "under the gun." Make the metronome one of the staples of your practice routine.

Quantizing: You Can Sound Better than You Are

Full-featured sequencing software and workstations have moderate- to highly-advanced quantizing capabilities. Quantizing is nothing but a fancy way of saying "rhythm correction." You choose the subdivisions of the beat you want to quantize to—one per beat (quarter note), two per beat (eighth notes), three per beat (triplet), four per beat (sixteenth notes), etc.—and the sequencer will snap your notes to the nearest subdivision of the beat, based on your settings. When using a sequencer's quantize function, you have to quantize to the smallest subdivision of the beat that was played. For instance, if the fastest notes of the sequenced part is four per beat (sixteenth notes), then the quantize grid has to be sixteenth notes. If you quantized to eighth notes, it would put two of the notes together as eighth notes (see fig. 8.3).

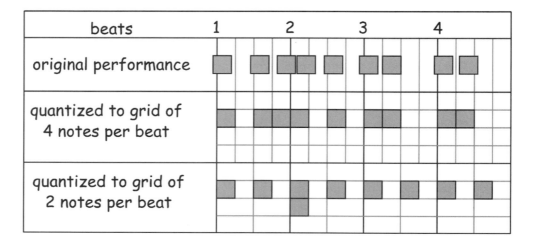

Fig. 8.3

You can quantize after you've finished inputting a performance, or as you're playing into a sequencer (input quantize). Quantizing is an extremely important and powerful sequencing tool. The way quantizing is used (or not) creates the feel of a drum track.

If I want a tight, rhythmically-correct dance drum track, I'll probably quantize every voice of the drum performance to a strict four notes-per-beat grid (sixteenth note). That is to say, if the sequencer divides the quarter note into 480 slices (the most common quarter-note beat resolution for sequencers), four evenly-spaced notes per beat (sixteenth notes, counted as "one-ee-and-ah") will fall at slices 0, 120, 240, and 360; each note is 120 slices long (slices are often called "ticks"). Notice that "zero" is "one" for the sake of quantization, the quarter note being broken into 480 values, numbered from 0-479.

The quantize feature allows you to select the resolution of the grid—from no quantization at all to almost any quantization value you can dream up. Fig. 8.4 shows an input quantization set to five notes (five per beat) in the time of four sixteenth notes (four per beat)—a five-let, or more accurately, a quintuplet. The notes will fall at ticks 0, 96, 192, 288, and 384. Oh, yeah—this rhythm could get you fired from most Top 40 drumming gigs, because dancers tend to fall down when they try to dance to such odd groupings. How cool would that be?

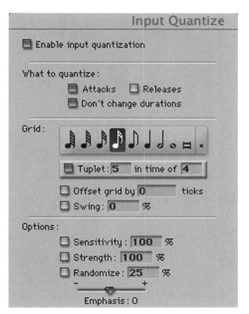

Fig. 8.4

TIP:
I learned to count a quintuplet aloud as "Da-la-pi-co-la," a takeoff on the name of the 20th century Italian composer Luigi Dallapiccola. This flows off the tongue well, and is simpler than "one-two-three-four-five." "Ta-ka, ta-ku-du" or "ta-ku-du, ta-ka" also work very well.

Experiment with quantization. Not only can you turn it off and play into the sequencer in real time, but you can vary the strength, sensitivity, and randomness of how quantizing is applied to a track. Use it to tighten the rhythm to varying degrees to create your perfect feel. Also, you might find it necessary to quantize just a note or two here and there, or just certain voices of the drum track, like the kick and snare, leaving the cymbals and toms with a looser feel. There are no hard and fast rules, and nothing is "wrong." How quantizing is used depends on how you want the finished track to sound and feel. The looseness or slop in our playing is what gives each drummer's playing a unique character. Don't always quantize that character out of drum sequences—make them musical!

The Keyboard Workstation as a Sequencer

Even if you rely on a computer and software to do most of your sequencing, it is more than likely that you or someone you work with has a keyboard workstation. A keyboard is a

workstation if it has the ability to sequence MIDI and play it back with onboard sounds. A keyboard, or any sound module for that matter, is multi-timbral when it can play back different sounds such as piano, bass, and drums at the same time, each on a separate MIDI channel. We've already experienced a workstation of sorts when we recorded into the TD-20's sequencer in an earlier chapter. It has six tracks, each with a different voice (sound) and MIDI channel. Almost every current drum module that has an onboard sequencer is multi-timbral. This feature allows you to produce drum sounds while playing along to a sequence from the same module.

At this writing, the Fantom-X workstation—really the X6, X7, and X8 models—is Roland's top-of-the-line keyboard workstation. It has tons of built-in sounds and room to expand to even more, with capability to add up to four 24-bit SRX expansion boards. It can also import loops and other audio samples via Compact Flash card or USB-to-computer hookup, and can seamlessly integrate these sounds with the factory sounds. If you don't have a computer and a sound source like a synth module, or computer software synthesizers (soft synths), a workstation would be a good choice to get started into sequencing. They have everything that is needed: a sequencer and multi-timbral sound source. The workstation offers the user sequencing without having to deal with more than a few pieces of gear. All it lacks are your great ideas!

Getting Started Is Easy

If you're going to be sequencing (inputting) drums using a keyboard workstation, it takes, at most, two MIDI cables to set up MIDI communication. In addition to routing MIDI, you'll also need to hear both the sounds generated by the keyboard and your drum module's sounds. (The keyboard may contain the other tracks you'll be playing to, such as bass and piano.) To hear everything,

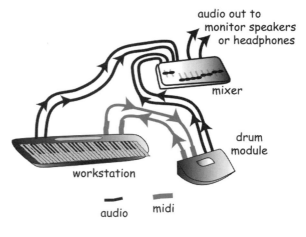

Fig. 8.5

you'll need to combine the audio from your drums and the audio from the workstation with a mixer (see fig. 8.5). That way, you can hear everything through the headphones. The only thing left to do is get a comfortable mix of the click, keyboard, and drums. Then you're off and sequencing!

TIP:
Remember correct audio and MIDI routing:
Always out-to-in, in-to-out. Never out-to-out, in-to-in.
It won't work, and may make a horrible sound!

Inputting a Few Notes to a Song:
Make It Red and Hit The drums!

Here we are, the moment you've been waiting for. We're going to sequence some notes! It's easy…

1. Set the number of count-off bars (look in the sequencer's manual).

2. Press the [Record] button (make it red).

3. Play some notes (in this case, we played just kick and snare).

4. Press the [Stop] button, then the [Rewind] button.

5. Press [Play]. If everything is plugged in correctly, you should hear exactly what you played. If not, check to see that all the cables are plugged into the correct places. Try again. Don't get frustrated. Troubleshooting is part of the learning process. I've made many mistakes, but they've all been part of the learning process.

TIP:
Playing your drums into a sequencer is not the only way to program a performance into it. You can get input performances by using the step input (may also be called "step pattern") function. You can enter a few notes at a time from the computer keyboard with perfect note values and velocities (volume). See the owner's manual for the lowdown on how to do this with your sequencer.

Let's Look at the Editing

The Song Edit screen of the Fantom-X6 is shown in fig. 8.6. Look at it closely. This screen shows the simple user interface of the X6's sequencer. Although the layout of other manufacturers' screens may differ, the information they contain will be much the same.

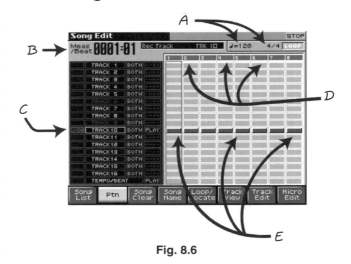

Fig. 8.6

I've labeled five important pieces of information shown on this screen (labeled A, B, C, D, E), material that we've previously covered, both in this chapter and in the chapter on MIDI. This information is the foundation of all sequencing, be it workstation or computer-based.

Fig. 8.6 (A) shows the tempo of the tune—in this case 120 BPM (beats per minute)—as well as the time signature of the sequence, four beats per measure. These can be changed to any of the common values. Tempo can be set to handle the slowest of ballads and the fastest of up-tempo tunes. Plus, you're not limited to just one tempo and meter per song—any number of tempo and meter changes can happen. This is especially true when working within software-based sequencing, where there is a tremendous amount of control over meter and tempo, even gradually slowing down and speeding up—just like some bass players!

Fig. 8.6 (B) is pointing to the numeric Measure/Beat display, which also shows where the sequencer will begin to play back (in this example at measure 1, beat 1, the downbeat of the first mesure of the sequence). Although it's currently at the beginning of the song, playback can begin from any point that's in the Measure/Beat display. This location is also referred to as the "current cursor position," and may be called the "insertion point." Still with me? Yes? Good.

The Fantom X6 gives us 16 tracks on which to record MIDI information. On the X6, MIDI Channels 1-16 are automatically assigned to Tracks 1-16, respectively. So, if we want to record (sequence) drums on MIDI Channel 10, the common MIDI channel for drums, we need to record on Track 10. This is almost ridiculously straight-ahead. Fig. 8.6 (C) shows that Track 10 is record-enabled. This is indicated by the "REC" symbol next to the track number. A track must be record-enabled before anything can be recorded onto it. Virtually any hardware or software, including digital audio workstations and tape, use this record-enable concept of arming a track for recording. After a track is armed (as another term for record-enabled) and the [Play] button is pressed, there's a one- or two-measure count off. Then you're sequencing drums. All that is left to do is play!

Fig. 8.6 (D) points to an overview of the measure numbers of the sequence. Here we can see eight mesures per screen, but the workstation (in fact, all sequencing software I've seen) allows you to zoom in or out to display fewer or more measures per screen. Zooming out is an easy way to get a complete view of a song's structure. Zooming in is useful when you want to see what's happening at a specific place, in a measure or in a beat. You'll use the zoom feature a great deal on both workstation- and computer software-based sequencers.

The dark rectangles that fig. 8.6 (E) points to show that there is MIDI data contained in those particular measures. The many different workstations and software programs have their own ways of indicating that a measure has data in it. Some sequencers even show how much data is in a measure by changing the color or the pattern of the rectangle as the amount of data increases. You have to love technology.

Before we start looking at the actual data on the drum track (Track 10), let's take a gander at the eight buttons along the bottom of the screen. They are the navigation and editing buttons, used to change the display to different edit screens. We're going to look at the Microscope screen. This screen will display the MIDI data of the selected track. In this case, oddly enough, it's the drum track. Ha!

Being at One with the MIDI Data

OK, remember that MIDI stuff we talked about last chapter? Well, we're about to use it. Welcome to Mike's Wild Ride. Please keep your hands and feet inside the car at all times.

The Fantom X6 Microscope screen, shown in fig. 8.7, is where you can see data on specific notes. All the values of the channel-voice message are found here: MIDI channel, note number, and velocity. In addition to this, there is some of the same information found on the Song Edit screen. Look at fig. 8.7 (A) and you'll see that Track 10

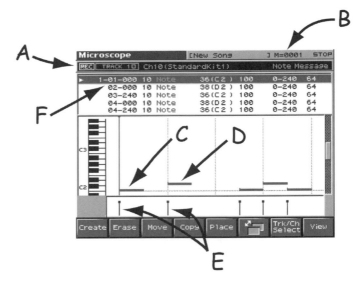

Fig. 8.7

is record-enabled. If you look at (B), the numeric display lets us know what measure number we're looking at on the screen (in this case, measure 1). Then there are the elements on the screen that we may be seeing for the first time, like that little vertical keyboard on the middle left. In sequencing, this has generically become known as the piano-roll view. The piano-roll view shows a lot of information about the individual MIDI notes (I'll simply call these "notes" from now on). First, the vertical lines to the right of the keyboard divide the bar into a quarter-note grid (four equal divisions). These make it easy to see where the notes fall against the beat. We can also see the pitches of the notes. Look at (C) and (D)—there are only two pitches shown, C2 and D2. These are the General MIDI Specification pitches for kick and snare. The notes fall on the beginning of beat 1 (kick), the beginning of beat 2 (snare), the upbeat of beat 3 (kick), the beginning of beat 4 (snare), and the upbeat of beat 4 (kick). What we have is a basic kick and snare rock beat:

1	&	2	&	3	&	4	&
kick	(rest)	snare	(rest)	(rest)	kick	snare	kick

It won't take long to learn to decipher this view and divine the rhythm from those little horizontal bars.

Fig. 8.7 (E) points to the velocity information for each note. Changing this data is self-explanatory—make the bar taller and the note will be louder; make the bar shorter and the note will be softer.

Now, if you're more comfortable with numbers, look at fig. 8.7 (F). It shows in text the note information we just looked at in a graphics format. This text view is sometimes referred to as an "event list." Both of these views can be found in almost every sequencing program. Let's look at the data (see fig. 8.7 (F)).

The first string of numbers, 01-01-000, shows that we're at measure 1, beat 1, tick 0 (remember, there are 480 ticks per beat: 0-479). The next number, 10, is the MIDI channel assignment for the note (and track). "Note" describes the kind of MIDI data—in this case, note data. The two pieces of data describe the note's pitch (note assignment) in two ways—as pitch and MIDI note number. If the General MIDI Specification is followed, the note number will tell you exactly what sound should be played—in this case 36 (kick), and 38 (snare). It is also shown by pitch and octave, C2 (the next octave up from C2 being C3, etc.).

The last three pieces of information are MIDI velocity (we musical types think of this as volume), a value of 100 here (127 max.), a note length of 240, which is the middle of the beat (240 ticks out of 480) and finally a note-off velocity of 64. Don't worry yet if you don't understand why there is a note length (sometimes called "gate time") and note-off velocity. The MIDI specification requires that a note-off command with note-off velocity be sent for every note-on command. Most drum modules ignore this information because drum sounds are relatively short and decay away naturally, rendering this note-off command unnecessary. In fact, most drum modules don't recognize either of these two pieces of information.

TIP:
Pitched synth sounds start playing with the note-on command and do not stop playing until after they receive note-off command. If you're triggering a pitched keyboard sound or other long sample, you will have to set the amount of time before the note-off command is sent (known as "gate time"). Otherwise, the note will continue to sound. Gate time is measured in milliseconds (ms). Drum and percussion sounds start playing with the note-on command and decay naturally, ignoring the note-off command.

Computer/Software Based Sequencing— Hey, Could You Check My Email?

We've just covered most of what there is to the basics of sequencing, so the next bit on computer-based sequencing will be painless. It'll be mostly the same information displayed in a different—some would say better and easier—way. I'll use both the Macintosh and PC computer platforms, using Digital Performer 5 by MOTU for the Mac and Sonar Producer 4.0 from Cakewalk for the PC. For the most part, I've used Macs since 1984. Now, after using PCs alongside my Macs, I've grown to appreciate that they have their place in the music workspace, too.

The first thing you'll notice about software-based sequencers is the enormous amount of information visible at a quick glance. Rather than looking at the small screen of the keyboard workstation, you now have the entire real estate of a computer display the information really wanted. This display can be as large as your computer graphics card and checkbook can handle. The different operating systems and the software used on the Mac and PC will each display the information a bit differently, but the type of information will be much the same. The way this data is displayed is entirely up to you. So, let's look at how the same information is displayed by Digital Performer on a Mac and Sonar Producer on the PC. I've had to shrink the graphics for each screen to fit on the page in the book, so if you have a hard time seeing the details, you can go to *http://mikesnyder.net/aaep* and navigate from there to the graphics page for this chapter. We live in a color world, and the screenshots posted on my website are much clearer than those printed here.

Fig. 8.8 and Fig. 8.9 show two complete screen images. Look at how the screens are laid out. They are made up of many different windows. The collection of windows visible at any one time is sometimes referred to as a "window set." You are able to create and save your own custom window sets. I have a number of different window sets saved, each geared toward different kinds of projects. For example, if I'm sequencing only MIDI, I'll use one set of windows. If I'm recording only digital audio, I'll use a different set. If I'm working on a project that requires both MIDI and digital audio, I'll use yet another window layout, perhaps even multiple window layouts.

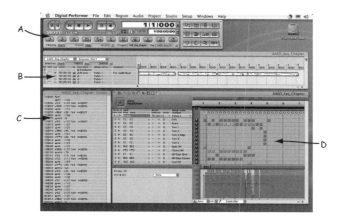

Fig. 8.8

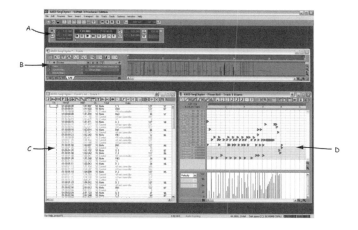

Fig. 8.9

There Seem to Be More Notes on These Screens!

In the earlier discussion on keyboard workstations, I limited the amount of data input to two notes, kick and snare, and the velocity information for those notes. The examples shown in fig. 8.8 and fig. 8.9 contain notes for a full-on drum set groove. This is so you can see what a complete drum pattern looks like in each of the different editing windows. The editing windows you decide to use are a matter of personal preference, and perhaps even habit. I used the event-list window for years before forcing myself to go to the drum editor and piano-roll views. It wasn't that the event list window was easier—in fact, using it was probably was harder and slower—but it was what I was used to, since this was the only screen view available for editing when I first began to use Performer (now Digital Performer) in the mid-1980s. Although I still use the event list window to do a lot of editing, I have begun to incorporate other editing windows, especially the drum edit view. OK, let's talk about the screenshots in more detail.

Hey, I Can See More Information on These Screens!

Fig. 8.8 and fig. 8.9 are screenshots of the main windows of two popular sequencing programs. Fig. 8.8 is from MOTU's Digital Performer program for the Macintosh platform, and fig. 8.9 is from Cakewalk's Sonar 3.0 Producer. The similar aspects of each of the two figures are labeled with letters A-D.

Fig. 8.8 and fig. 8.9 (A) show the large transport controls, which are used to navigate around the measures of a sequence. I'll say more about those shortly.

Track View is shown in fig. 8.8 and fig. 8.9 (B). This is comparable to the Song Edit window in the Fantom X6's sequencer that we looked at earlier. The difference with these track windows—all the windows for that matter—is that the amount of information you can view is limited only to the size of your monitor. The larger the monitor, the more you can see. This window also includes the input and output information for the MIDI and audio found on each track and information on what patch the sound module should be using. I suggest that this window should always be open, as it functions as an overview window.

Fig. 8.8 and fig. 8.9 (C) show the Event List window, which, as we've seen before, contains the track's MIDI data in text form. Notice that a lot more information is shown here. The data displayed in these windows is user-customizable. The default settings are shown.

The data shown in fig. 8.8 and fig. 8.9 (D) is in a new format. The Drum Editor view is to look at non-pitch drum track data. At the left of each window, you can see the name of the instrument each note number represents. Right out of the box, these sequencing programs will list the General MIDI instrument names for the note values. If there are any differences with the instrument assignments for drums you're using, you can rename any of the note numbers. Look closely at fig. 8.8 (D). You'll see that there are four notes assigned for the hi-hat, which definitely is not General MIDI standard. This is because I used the Roland V-Pro Series TD-20S drums that have the VH-12 hi-hats. These hi-hats have two cymbals, just like acoustic hi-hats, and send much more information than the standard pad and FD foot controller.

⠿⠿⠿ Transport Me Up, Scotty!

One of the first things you will notice is the large transport controls. Not only can you arm the sequencer for recording, but you'll also find controls for tempo and meter rewinding, as well as access to many of the program's setup features like MIDI setup, audio setup (we'll discuss that later), and window view selection. Look at fig. 8.10 and fig. 8.11. They show in detail the transport controls for both Digital Performer and Sonar.

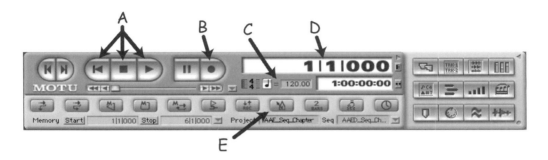

Fig. 8.10. Digital Performer (Mac)

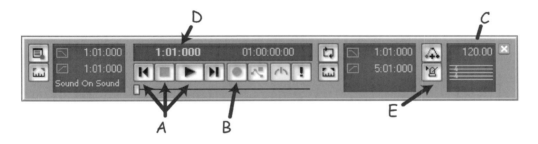

Fig. 8.11. Sonar (PC)

ALL ABOUT ELECTRONIC PERCUSSION

The similar functions of each transport control are labeled with letters and listed below. Notice how the same functions are displayed slightly differently on each transport screen.

    A. [Rewind], [Stop], and [Play], respectively

    B. [Record Enable]

    C. [Tempo]

    D. [Current Cursor Position], Measure, Beat, and Number of Ticks

    E. [Meter]

Again, same information, different layout...

OK, We're All In Order...

There you have it, a general introduction to sequencers. All the different sequencers do the same thing. Although their basic information is all the same, the look and feel of each user interface can be vastly different. Consider a sequencer's user interface when choosing your primary sequencing application. Pick one that's easy on your eyes, as you'll spend countless hours looking at it. Do your research and ask people in the know lots of questions. Remember, there are no dumb questions. So, go forth and jump into the world of sequencing.

For further information visit:

    http://rolandus.com

    http://edirol.com

    http://cakewalk.com

    http://motu.com

And of course:

    http://mikesnyder.net

NINE

A SAMPLING PRIMER

Sampling: The Basics

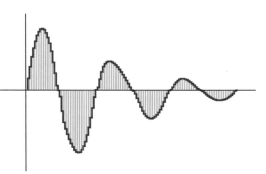

So far in this book, there has been a great deal of discussion about sound and how it relates to electronic drums and percussion. We've learned how to manipulate sounds using the latest sound modeling technology that's found in some drum modules, discussed the sound formats used in today's hard disk recorders, and touched on some of the popular music software titles. We've also covered how audio is output from sound modules, as well as how this audio is manipulated, amplified, and recorded. Eventually, you might run across a situation where you're going to want to create and play your own sounds, have a need to play a sound effect or other sound that's not found on your electronic drum module, or create a completely new sound that exists only in your head. This is where sampling becomes the technology of need.

The technology to sample sound, to create a digital representation of an analog sound, has been on the consumer market for some 25 years. I bought my first sampler in the late 1980s. It had the incredible ability to sample about 14 seconds of stereo sound at a quality that wasn't even near that of an audio CD—but it cost over $3000 (USD). Today, there is a sampler out there, the Roland SPD-S Sample Pad, which potentially has

Fig. 9.1

hours of CD-quality sampling, and costs less than $600 (USD) (see fig. 9.1). Every drummer should have one. In less than 20 years, the technology has advanced from being able to sample and store a few short sounds and loops to having numerous complete songs, dozens of loops, and a myriad of single-hit sounds on a memory card that costs only about as much as a decent lunch... and at CD quality.

Exactly What Is Sampling?

As I said earlier, sampling is the act of making a digital representation of an analog sound. It is occasionally referred to as "digitizing a sound," Take a look at fig. 9.2. It shows the signal flow when sampling an analog sound. A sound is played into a sampler from a

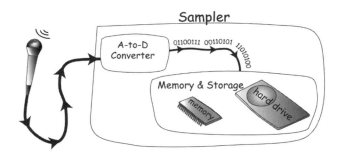

Fig. 9.2

source of audio. This source could be a CD player, a direct input from a line-level instrument (like a guitar or synth), or a signal from a microphone. Whatever the audio source, the path is the same. The audio is fed into a chip called an analog-to-digital converter, commonly referred to as an A-to-D converter. This chip turns the audio into a binary representation: zeros and ones, bits and bites. This digitized sound, now officially called a "sample", is saved onto some sort of storage device (such as a hard drive or a memory card) so that it can be recalled and played at a later time. The sound can be stored in several different sound formats, the most popular ones being AIFF (originally a Mac format), WAV (originally a Windows PC format), and MP3. See the chapter on looping for an in-depth discussion of sound file formats.

Look at fig. 9.3. When a sample is recalled for playback (its pad is hit), it goes through the reverse of the sampling process and is sent back through a digital-to-analog converter (D-to-A converter). The D-to-A converter turns the sample back into an analog signal and sends it to the sampler's audio outputs so

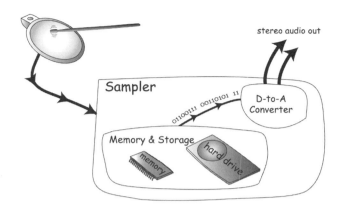

Fig. 9.3

that they can be heard. Both the A-to-D and D-to-A converters process the sample very quickly, so there is virtually no delay from when the pad is hit to when you hear the sound.

So, that was pretty painless, wasn't it?

Going Analog-to-Digital: What You Need to Know

As I noted earlier, a sample is a digital representation of an analog sound. Let's see what a sample looks like, and how it compares to its analog brother.

Any analog sound can be represented by a waveform that contains all the sound's information: frequency, length, and dynamic range (volume). A sound can have frequency information as simple as that of a sine

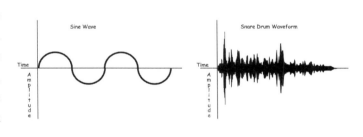

Fig. 9.4

wave (see fig. 9.4 left), or as complex as that of a snare drum hit (see fig. 9.4 right). Whereas sound length is rather simple to represent digitally, there are two factors—sample rate and bit depth—that affect both frequency and dynamic range. They help determine how closely the digital sample matches the original analog sound.

Sample Rate

The sample rate is the number of times per second a snapshot is taken of a sound's amplitude; each of these snapshots is called a sample. Fig. 9.5 shows a simple, smooth analog waveform (in black) and

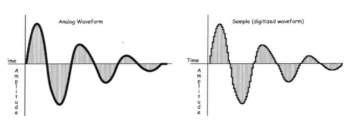

Fig. 9.5

the snapshots (in grey) taken of the waveform. When the sampling process is finished, you can see that the originally smooth wave now has a staircase appearance; it is a digital representation of the original analog sound, a sample. Notice that the sample closely resembles the shape of the analog waveform, but not quite exactly. A sound's sample rate directly affects the quality of the sound. The higher the sample rate, the smaller the stair steps will be. The smaller the stair steps, the closer the sampled sound will be to the original smooth analog wave.

To illustrate, fig. 9.6 shows a waveform before and after being sampled—first with a low sample rate, then with a much higher sample rate. As you can see, the wave with the higher sample rate more

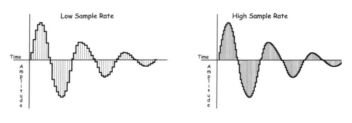

Fig. 9.6

closely resembles the original analog waveform. The choice of sample rate also dictates how much of a sound's high-end frequency can be reproduced in the sample. Yes, it involves math. But rest assured, there won't be a pop quiz later on.

Sample Rate, Frequencies, and the Audio CD

The sample rate of an audio CD is 44.1K. In other words, there are 44,100 snapshots, or samples, per second. This is not just some arbitrary number pulled out of thin air by some engineer type when the CD standard was being developed. This rate is based on a mathematical theorem called Nyquist's Theorem and on the average range of human hearing. Simply put, Nyquist's Theorem postulates that the highest frequency that can be reproduced by a sampled sound is about half the sample rate. So, audio CDs have a sample rate of 44.1K. Half of that is 22.05K. This means that a CD can reproduce frequencies up to around 22.05 Hz; it just so happens that this is near the top end of a human's (non-guitar player) range of hearing.

When CDs were being developed, the technology available to store large amounts of data was less sophisticated, and considerably more expensive than it is today. Because of those factors, the engineers went with the minimum sample rate needed to cover our full spectrum of hearing. The choice was a balance between cost and function. Today, storage is inexpensive, so we now see sample rates of 96K (DVDs), 192K (high-end hard disk recorders), and even higher. Some people make the argument that we can't hear the increased high frequencies that higher sample rates can reproduce, but when you compare lower and higher sample rates side-by-side, there is a noticeable difference.

Bit Depth

The other variable in making samples sound better is bit depth. While sample rate determines the high frequencies that can be reproduced, bit depth determines the number of vertical steps used to represent the amplitude of a waveform. The amplitude of a waveform determines its dynamic range (volume). It just so happens that the higher the bit depth, the lower a sample's noise floor. For reference, an audio CD uses 16 bits to represent amplitude, most hard disk recorders use 24 bits, and some music hardware and software even use 64 bits. You'll hear the effects of a low bit depth primarily at low volumes, like the fade-outs at the end of songs. If you listen very closely, you might hear the volume stair step down at the very end of the fade. That's because there are few vertical numbers used to represent amplitude as the volume decreases. That being said, the higher the bit depth, the less there will be of this effect.

Fig. 9.7 shows two copies of the same sound that were sampled at the same sample rate, but at differing bit depths. For the sake of illustration, the first has a bit depth of 16 bits (64 levels, +32 and -32),

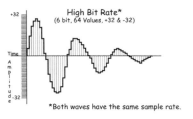
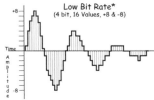

*Both waves have the same sample rate.

Fig. 9.7

and -32), and the second has a bit depth of four bits (16 levels, +8 and -8). Although the waves are sampled at the same sample rate—each of the examples contains 106 samples—the wave (sample) with the higher bit rate has less stair stepping, and is smoother overall (see fig. 9.7 left). The effect of how a low bit rate will make samples—especially the low-volume portion—sound "unnatural" can be seen by the extremely squared-off end of the low bit rate sample in (see fig. 9.6 right). Notice that the fade is much smoother on the first sample with the higher bit depth.

Although the examples we've just been through involve bit rates of just six and four (64 & 16 levels, respectively), "real life" examples will start at 16 bits (almost 66,000 levels), and go up from there. I couldn't get my pencil sharp enough to begin to draw that many levels!

> *TIP:*
> *If you recall the discussion of bits in the chapter on MIDI, you know that eight bits (a Byte) can represent 256 values. Remember, with each added bit, the number of possible values doubles. So, if eight bits can represent 256 values (2^8), 16 bits can represent 65,536 values (2^{16}), and 24 bits can represent a whopping 16,777,216 value (2^{24})!*

Let's stop the math lesson here... before I make your head explode. Simply let me say that the higher the bit depth, the better the sample will sound. Simple, direct, and to the point.

The SPD-S: Sampling Made Easy

While it's good to have all this background information about sampling, Roland's SPD-S Sampling Pad makes sampling and editing your own sounds very easy. I guess they figure that we're drummers, and probably not card-carrying members of MENSA. What's that? You're not? OK then, perhaps they were right.

The SPD-S is a compact, nine-pad, two-trigger input percussion controller. Because it is a sampling pad, you're not limited only to the sounds that are

The Roland SPD-S Sample Pad

stored in memory at the factory. You can add your own sounds, be they one-shot sounds or loops. Out of the box from the factory, the SPD-S has enough memory for approximately six minutes of CD-quality samples and places to store and name 399 samples. These samples can be as short as a cowbell hit or as long as an entire song. The beauty is, you decide.

> *TIP:*
> *In contrast to the SPD-S Sampling Pad, sounds are stored very differently in other percussion pads like the Roland SPD-20 and Handsonic. The SPD-20 and Handsonic contain sounds that are permanently stored in memory called ROM (Read-Only Memory). Although they can be edited and manipulated, they cannot be erased; they are burned into the chips. On the other hand, the SPD-S stores its sounds in "flash memory," memory that can easily be erased, reallocated, and reused.*

Getting Samples into the SPD-S

In my opinion, the SPD-S is the easiest-to-use sampler on the market today. But don't let its size and ease of use mislead you—it is a very advanced sampler, one capable of advanced sample manipulation. Even though it is very advanced, much of the power is presented in a way that is clear, simple, and concise. This section is not intended to be a user manual for the SPD-S—refer to its owner's manual and available online help for that. It's meant to help you get a general overview of the SPD-S sample process. Let's take a look.

The SPD-S comes loaded with approximately 181 sounds that cover a wide range of drums, percussion, loops, and pitched (non-drum) sounds. I chose to keep those sounds and expand the memory with a Compact Flash memory card, and I would suggest that you do the same. Compact Flash cards are inexpensive, so get either a 256 MB or 512 MB card (the operating system for the SPD-S will accept up to a 512 MB card). Insert the card into the slot on the side, and use the card utilities on the SPD-S to format the card. Then you're off and sampling.

Getting the Samples Sound In

There are two approaches to getting a sound into the SPD-S: using the audio inputs on the back of the SPD-S or editing the sound on a computer and transferring it via a Compact Flash card to the SPD-S. While some people prefer the simplicity of using the SPD-S to sample and edit, others like editing on the computer because you can see the waveform on the screen. Both work.

Sampling Using Just the SPD-S

Fig. 9.8 shows the audio inputs on the back of the SPD-S that are used for sampling. The source of the sound can be almost anything, from an audio CD player output (line level), to a microphone or two (mic level). If you are going to sample in stereo, use both of the audio inputs. If you are going to sample in mono, use only the input

Fig. 9.8

marked "L (MONO)." The SPD-S senses whether or not there is something plugged in the second (R) input; if there is, it will attempt to sample in stereo. There is a switch next to the inputs to toggle between mic or line level.

> *TIP:*
> *When deciding whether to sample in stereo or in mono, consider the following: stereo samples not only use additional memory, they also diminish the number of sounds that can be played at one time (polyphony) by half. For example, while you may want backing tracks to be in stereo, a sample of a single cowbell hit will sound just fine in mono. If you're not sure, sample it in mono.*

After plugging the audio into the back of the SPD-S, follow the directions in the owner's manual to sample the sound. With the SPD-S, the sampling can be done with as few as four button pushes, and all the buttons you need to use will light up and flash as they're needed. One of the intuitive things the SPD-S does is prompt you to assign a sound to one of the pads, pedals, or trigger inputs as part of the sampling process. So, when you're finished sampling, you are very close to being ready to perform.

OK, So You Want to Do Some Editing, Huh?

Invariably, you'll want to do some editing of a sample. This could include leveling out the sample's volume so that it better blends with other samples, or making a sample loop repeat, or loop evenly (see the chapter on looping for an in-depth discussion). This can be done by adjusting the start point and end point of the loop until it repeats smoothly. You can also tell the SPD-S whether you want the sample to loop (repeat) or be one-shot (play only once).

> *TIP:*
> *One of the great things the SPD-S can do is take loops of differing tempos and synchronize them to a common master tempo. Although the SPD-S makes this seem easy, it requires very advanced technology.*

Putting the Computer in the Loop (Pun Intended)

Having been a self-professed computer geek for some 20 years, I make use of my computer to do certain types of editing before I transfer the sample(s) to the SPD-S. Quite frankly, making loops repeat perfectly, and evening-out sample volumes with gain change or normalizing is much easier when you use a

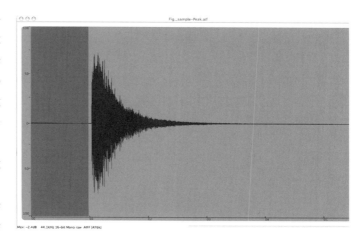

Fig. 9.9

computer and sound-editing software. Fig. 9.9 shows a single hi-hat hit as it appears in the sound editing software Peak from Bias, Inc. When editing samples on the SPD-S, you have to listen for the extra space and noise before the actual sample. With Peak, you can actually see it (see fig. 9.9) and, better yet, delete it.

Once all the editing is done on the computer, copy the file (.AIF or .WAV format) to the root directory of the Compact Flash card (see fig. 9.10). Take the card out of the computer, insert it into the card slot on the SPD-S and use the card utilities to import the sample into the SPD-S. After that, you'll have to manually assign the sound to a pad within a patch. The SPD-S imports the sample into a Roland proprietary format with the

Fig. 9.10

suffix of SPD. Because of this format, we're able do things such as synchronize the sample to a master tempo, change its pitch without changing its tempo, change its tempo without changing its pitch, and easily add effects. Isn't life grand?

The SPD-S: A Sample Pad for Every Drummer

I think that the SPD-S is a piece of electronic gear that every drummer should own. It functions well as a sound source off to the side of acoustic drums, giving the drummer easy access to any kind of sound imaginable. It's also a great way to ease oneself into the world of looping, because as we saw with the importing of external sounds from the computer via Compact Flash, you can just as easily export a sound from the SPD-S back to the computer as an .AIF or .WAV file. This makes it very easy to trade samples back and forth with other people. The SPD-S also has a dual-mono trigger input, so you can add pads or triggers to your acoustic drum set—great if you want to plug in an acoustic drum trigger and fatten up your kick drum sound with a terrific-sounding sample.

TEN

LOOPING
Software-Based Looping

I don't remember exactly why and when I made my first loop. I think perhaps it was some kind of percussion loop for a long-forgotten horror film in the mid-1980s. The final resting place for this loop was an Akai S1000 sampler. That loop (and many others) is still around on a 3.5" floppy in a dusty case. (Note to self: throw some stuff out.) This was the beginning of my life as Loop Boy.

This chapter will give you the basics for creating drum and percussion loops. The process by which you'll end up making loops is a determined by the hardware and software you're using, and the style of music in which the loops will be used.

Much of today's popular music uses drum loops. A composer might use a loop as inspiration while writing a song, or there might be a loop used in a song's final production. Either way, loop content creation is a growing way to earn a living. It's another part of what we are expected to do as working drummers, so spend some time behind the computer working on your mouse chops.

It is important to listen to a lot of music that uses loops. These days, that's almost every kind of popular music out there. This will help you develop an ear for how loops are used, and what kind of sounds are currently in vogue. At times, it can be difficult to distinguish what combination of sounds you're hearing. Is what you're hearing a loop, programmed drums, electronic drums, acoustic drums, or some combination of all the above? Have faith. Eventually you'll develop the ability to dissect all the different parts. If you have friends or acquaintances who are currently using loops in their live or recorded music, pick their brains, hang out, and learn as much as you can. Practical real-life experience is priceless.

Things to Consider when Looping

First, think about how the loop will be used. Will it be a one-bar loop, a two-bar loop, or a loop set of twelve parts? Consider how the finished loop will be used. Is it for live performance? A song demo? A CD project? A jingle? This puts me into a particular mode of working. For instance, a jingle will probably have a limited budget when compared to a union record session. A larger budget means that most likely there will be more time to spend on the loop production. I've seen big budget records sessions spend a day on a single two-bar loop. On the other side of the coin, I've walked into jingle sessions and walked out ten minutes later, the project finished. Most often, the client will have recorded examples of what they think they want. This is especially true on jingles, which have a "temp" track of music the producer has fallen in love with, but doesn't want—or can't afford—to license.

The second consideration is a musical one. What style do the loops need to be? They could be some kind of techno thing, open alternative slosh, or who knows what. You have to be prepared to deal with any eventuality. In my L.A. studio days, there was more than one time that I told the contractor I had an instrument I didn't even know existed, let alone owned. Such is life. Take some chances, but be prepared for anything!

The third deals with the technical side. What is the recording format? It could be anything from stand-alone hard disk recorder, to 2" tape. Is it Roland's VS-Series hard-disk recorders, computer-based hard disk recording such as Pro Tools or Digital Performer, or will it be tape? Some or all of these formats might be used.

Then there are the parameters that make the budding loopmaker shake with fear and bite the end of their pencil: sound file format, sample rate, and bit depth.

Sound File Format

For newcomers to digital audio, sound file format is perhaps the biggest challenge. Audio sound files are recognized by the three or four digit suffix (.xxx) after the file name.

The following are some of the common formats:

AIF– Audio Interchange Format

This is a computer file format. AIF is most commonly found on Macintosh computers, but most Windows programs can read these files as well. They can be mono, split stereo, or stereo interleaved files. Split stereo files contain two separate but linked files whose name ends in ".L" and ".R". Interleaved files show up as one stereo file. This format can embed "loop points" in the file. This file is capable of most sample rates and bit depths.

SDII– Sound Designer II Format

This file format, pioneered by Digidesign, is similar to AIF. Stereo files in this format are commonly split stereo (two mono sound files that make up one stereo file), but may also be interleaved.

WAV– Microsoft Windows Audio Format

This is a computer file format that was first associated with Windows PCs. It can contain marker information, but not loop points. This file is capable of all sample rates and bit depths, and can be a mono or stereo file.

MP3

This highly compressed audio format is commonly used in Web and multimedia presentations, as well as portable audio players. Its files are about one-tenth the size of the same length AIF and WAV files.

RX2

This is the format used in the Recycle software from Propellerheads. It contains imbedded "slice" information that allows you to stretch and compress a file without changing the pitch. It also contains MIDI information about the timing of the slices that certain software programs can import, thus making changing the feel of the loop much easier.

Sample Rate

Sample rate is the number of times per second a sound has a snapshot taken of its waveform. CD quality is 44.1K, or 44,100 snapshots per second. Half the sample rate is roughly the highest frequency that a given sample rate can represent. The 44.1K sample rate was chosen because it can represent frequencies of up to c22K, which covers the complete human audible hearing range (for most of us, anyway).

Common Sample Rates:

22.05K - Multimedia & Web presentations
44.1K - Audio CDs
48K - Video production
96K - DVDs

Bit Depth

Bit depth is the number of binary zeros and ones used to describe each snapshot. The more bits, the more accurately the sound is reproduced. Although audio CDs use 16-bits, 24-bit is now the common recording standard. It just sounds better. The higher the number of bits used, the wider the dynamic range of the sound.

Hardware

With the vast array of hardware and software available, there is no set way to approach looping. It's a matter of what the people you work with are using, what technical support is readily available, and budget.

Back when I first started creating loops (hand me my arthritis medicine, please), the music technology available for creating and editing loops made the process somewhat complex and time consuming. There were no CD-quality hard disk recorders and very little sound editing software. Personal computing power was limited and expensive. Loops were created and sampled into stand-alone samplers and were edited by numbers that represented samples per second. All this has changed drastically in the last ten years. We now have inexpensive, high-quality gear that makes the recording and looping process much easier.

My looping setup is simple. Depending on the client, I'll use either a Roland VS-Series standalone hard-disk recorder or a Macintosh computer with a Mark of the Unicorn firewire audio interface. Both setups are similar in cost.

As to what kind of gear to purchase, find a balance between the predominant recording formats your peers are using and your comfort level with computers. The Roland VS-Series recorders are truly studios in a box. They have built-in microphone preamps, expandable effects, and motorized faders. Put sound in and out pops a finished audio CD. When you plug a video monitor, keyboard, and mouse into these recorders, the lines between computers and stand-alone hard disk recorders become blurred. Standalone hard-disk recorders are the only choice if you're computer-phobic. Plus, I've never seen a VS recorder crash. I wish I could say that for computers.

I've been a computer geek seemingly forever. My first computer was an Apple Macintosh I bought in March 1984, and I have owned several Macs since. A dual processor G5 and the MotU audio interface are the basis of my current computer hard-disk recording system. There are good PC-based recording systems out there, but I admit that I'm biased.

To deliver the finished loops, you'll need to have a CD-R or DVD-R. Most new computers come standard with at least one of these drives. Alternatively, you can email or FTP the finished loops to the client.

Beyond one or both of the above systems, you'll need some sort of speakers to monitor your audio. Don't use stereo speakers! There are plenty of great inexpensive studio monitors available, both powered and unpowered. With studio monitors, you'll hear what's going on with the sound more accurately.

There are less expensive pieces of gear that are available to get your feet wet in looping. Although I won't discuss these in depth, check out the Roland SPD-S Sample Pad, a lot of power for not-much money.

Software

Discussion of software is mainly the realm of the computer-based systems. Although all stand-alone recorders use software, which in most cases can be updated, it is relatively transparent to the user. Not so with computers. The world of music software for computers has exploded in the last few years. Much of what was done with hardware in the past is now done with a computer and software.

With computer-based recording systems, you need both hardware and software to make them run. Because I've been using versions of this software for over 20 years, I use Mark of the Unicorn's Digital Performer for my digital audio and MIDI recording. There's no sense in learning a new program unless you have to. Digital Performer is a Macintosh-only program that has done a great job of seamlessly blending both the digital audio and the MIDI aspects of computer-based recording. Other programs integrate MIDI and digital audio well. These include Apple's Logic and Cakewalk's Sonar. Digidesign's Pro Tools is arguably the most widely-accepted digital recording format, but it lacks elegant integration of MIDI.

Even though all the above programs contain tools to create and edit loops, I use a Mac-only audio editing program called Peak (from Bias, Inc.) to do my final loop editing. It can import and export most audio formats and apply EQ and effects. But its greatest feature is called Loop Surfer™, which lets you set a beginning and ending loop point based on number of beats and tempo, then actively drag this "loop grid" around to any point in the audio file—while the file is playing! This makes finding a good loop point easy. Loop Surfer has saved me a great deal of time and is worth the price of the program alone. There are similar products available for PCs. Consult your local digital audio guru for more information.

Although the above software is all that is needed to create crushing loops, two other great programs can drastically modify existing loops, as well as create loops completely inside your computer. Because songwriters can go to the "loop well" only so many times, there's a program called Recycle from Propellerheads. This program allows you to change the tempo of a loop without changing the pitch or to change the pitch without changing the tempo, among many other things. None of this could be done without computer technology. A program called Reason, also from Propellerheads, is a blast to use and can get you creating in different ways. Hey, let's make some loops…

Loop Creation: An Example

When recording drums—or any instrument for that matter—make sure there is a good strong level on each track. This is true for analog (tape) recordings, as well as digital recordings. You want to get the level as loud (hot) as possible without the sound distorting. Analog distortion doesn't sound very good and digital distortion is even worse. You'll know it when you hear it! The hotter the recorded level, the better the signal-to-noise ratio and the wider the dynamic range. Digitally recorded files can always be normalized, a process that raises a sound file's level to near maximum without distorting it. This is something you can do if you have to use sound files with low-recorded levels, but it is not the best course of action. A level of 75 to 100 percent of maximum is best (see fig. 10.1).

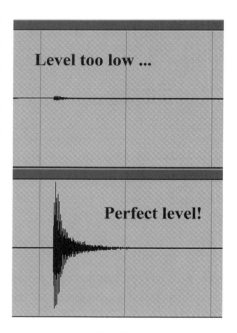

Level too low …

Perfect level!

Fig. 10.1

Because the V-Drums have eight audio outputs, recording them is much like recording acoustic drums, but without much of the hassle. For these loops, the audio is split out into seven outputs: kick, snare, stereo cymbals, hi-hat, and stereo toms. The stereo cymbal and tom pairs contain panning information. For example, the four toms take up only two tracks on a recorder, but their audio still moves gradually from one side to the other, depending on how they are panned. To accomplish this with acoustic drums, you would have to use four microphones and four tracks on a recorder.

Fig. 10.2 shows the four main windows used for navigation and editing in Digital Performer (hereafter referred to as DP). "A" contains the transport controls and information about the current file. This information includes some of the things we talked about earlier. Just to the right of middle of this window you'll see the sample rate

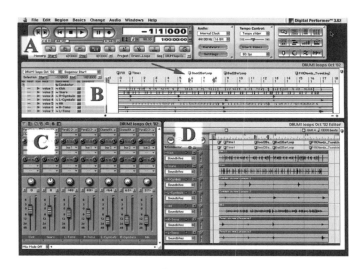

Fig. 10.2

and bit depth with which this DP file is recorded: 44.1K sample rate and 16-bit depth. Looks like CD quality to me.

The individual MIDI and audio tracks are found here in window "B," but since there are no MIDI tracks, you see only an audio overview. The ability to edit audio and MIDI together in this window is where DP shines. Window "C" is the mixing board. You add effects, EQ, etc. here. "D" is the audio-editing window. This is where you can edit the individual tracks. You have the ability to slice up the audio, move it around, and even replace notes. If a section of the recording is a great-sounding loop, but there is a snare hit (or any other sound) that seems bad, you can find a another hit in the recording, copy it, and replace the bad one. If you look at window "C" of fig. 10.2, you can see that I've already done the mix for these drum tracks: panned things, changed volume levels with the faders, and added EQ and effects. This is all standard drum-mixing stuff.

I've recorded 18 measures of drum groove with the hope of getting at least one two-measure loop, and perhaps a fill or two. Recording more material than you need gives the tempo a chance to settle down and increases the odds you'll find a good loop point. Steadiness of tempo and subtle changes in drum and cymbal sounds are two things that affect how well an acoustic loop sounds when repeating on itself. More electronic-sounding loops have less of this problem because the sounds are inherently more consistent. The time aspect is obvious, but if the sound changes color too much, you'll begin to hear the repetitiveness of the loop. The shorter the loop, the more obvious the repetitiveness tends to be. There are times that this can be a cool sound, but most of the time it isn't.

While listening through the second time, I use the DP's "marker" feature to label the good spots and bad spots (the arrow in fig. 10.2 "B" points to four markers). These markers list possible places to grab a couple of fills, a two-measure loop that works well, and even a marker that points to some not-very-tight playing on my part. Keeping track of the measure numbers of the good and bad spots saves a lot of editing time later on when the final loop editing is being done in Peak. Use the repeat feature in DP to audition possible bars for looping. The arrow in fig. 10.2 "B" points to the internal two-measure repeat I've set up in DP to hear how bars six and seven loop around on themselves As it turns out, these measures sound great, both musically and sonically. This will be the two-measure loop we'll isolate in Peak. The fills will come from the very first measure and measures 15–16.

Mixing is an educated guessing game when you're doing it without the other band parts. My experience has shown me that the low end of the drum mix needs to be louder and have more punch than one would think. Otherwise, when the loop is used in a song, it'll be too thin. When mixing, reference CDs with similar drum sounds, as well as drum sounds you like.

After all this listening and marking, I mix all the tracks down to a stereo file by bouncing all the tracks to disk. (Remember, DP uses "split stereo" files as its sound format.) Now it's time to open the stereo mix in Peak.

Using Peak to Bring Loops Some Love

With source measures already identified in DP, we use Peak to do any needed surgery on the loop to make it sound, feel, and loop better. Be careful though— it's possible to edit and correct the life right out of the loop. Little pushes and pulls in tempo are what we use to create great "feels" and give our grooves character. Editing loops is a tap dance between making the loop rhythmically tight and not killing the groove entirely.

Fig. 10.3 shows the complete raw mix in Peak. The loop we defined earlier at measures 6 and 7 is selected with Peak's Loop Surfer feature. Since we already know the two-measure loop we want starts at measure 6, I listened to the mix from the beginning and stopped playback right at the downbeat. Then I expanded the loop waveform around the downbeat of measure 6, and placed the cursor right at the beginning of the waveform (see fig. 10.4). After opening up Loop Surfer, you can plug in the number of beats (eight), and tempo (88bpm) and a perfect loop endpoint is insert by Peak (see fig. 10.5). Voilà! We have a perfectly timed loop, right down to the sample. Our parents would be proud.

Now the loop is selected and pasted into a new stereo file containing only the selected loop. This loop is almost done, but not quite. You see it's a two-measure loop, and we have to see if it will loop well on itself at a one-measure loop length. We can take this further and see if it will also loop well at two beats, and even one beat. You can edit all the way down to the sample level with Peak. When you're satisfied with the fruits of your loop labor, save the loop in the sound file format you need, repeat for any other loops needed, and you're done.

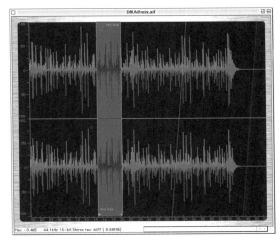

Fig. 10.3

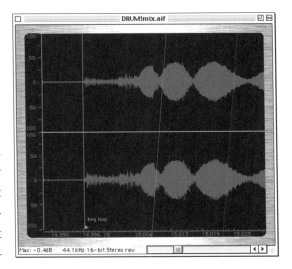

Fig. 10.4

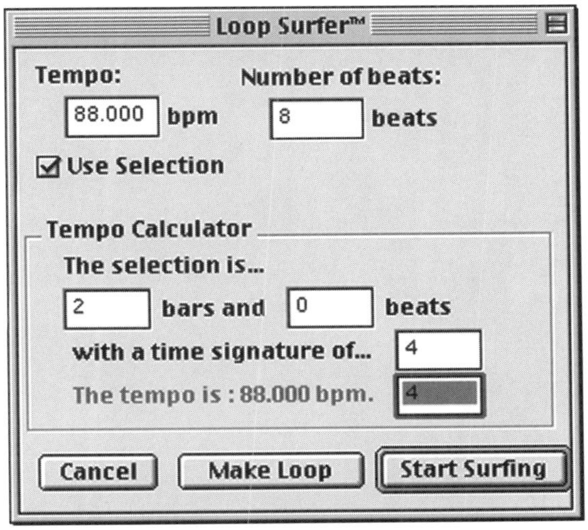

Fig. 10.5

Outro

These days, all bets are off as to what is a good or a bad drum sound. Some of my coolest loops were done with a funky old microphone normally used as talk-back mic in the drum booth. Experiment! Create as many loops as possible—every groove, style, and drum sound is valid. It's just like practicing rudiments—the more you do it, the better you get.

The raw stereo file and finished loops can be found at:

http://mikesnyder.net/aaep/looping

Other Links:

http://rolandus.com for VS-Series hard-disk recorders and V-Drums

http://bias-inc.com for Peak

http://www.propellerheads.se for Recycle and Reason

http://motu.com for information on Digital Performer

ELEVEN

TRIGGERING FROM ACOUSTIC DRUMS

Back to School: Triggering 101

As drummers and percussionists, the tools that are available today to us are nothing sort of wondrous. From high quality, great-sounding acoustic drums to the ability to integrate the use of electronics and computers into our everyday practice and performance, the past ten years have brought us a varied array of new and improved technologies. While triggering electronics from acoustic drums has been around for over 20 years, triggering hardware continues to improve. So, spit out the gum and let's go to school!

 Ready, Aim, Trigger

We've grown accustomed to the great drum sounds we hear on recorded music. As drummers, we are expected to reproduce quality sounds whenever we perform. The bar is higher than it has ever been. The problem is, great drum sounds take an experienced engineer and a bunch of very expensive gear to create—and more than likely, it's gear and expertise we don't posses. Pass the drum triggers, please...

The concept of triggering acoustic drums is actually quite simple. When using drum triggers on your acoustic drums, the drum trigger/acoustic drum combination takes the place of the electronic drum pad. Simple, right? Some of you are probably saying to yourself, "OK, but I'm an acoustic guy who breaks out in a rash when I plug in the vacuum cleaner. Help me. Exactly how do I trigger my acoustic drums?" Well, let me educate you.

Triggering: The Terminology

Let's define some basic terminology so that we're talking the same language. Refer to fig. 11.1 while reviewing the following terminology.

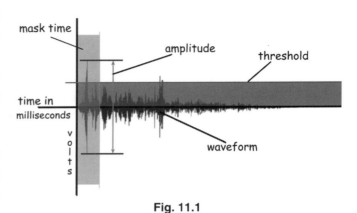

Fig. 11.1

Waveform: the representation of the voltage output of a drum trigger; shown in amplitude over time

Amplitude: the height of the waveform; measured in volts

Sensitivity: a trigger interface setting used balance out the varying voltage output levels of different acoustic triggers and pads

Velocity Curve: a trigger interface setting used to alter how a sound module's sound output volume changes in relation to user input

Mask Time: the amount of time a trigger input waits before it will react to another trigger waveform; generally measured in milliseconds

Millisecond: a measurement of time; one second equals 1000 milliseconds (ms; in air, sound travels at the rate of about one foot per millisecond

Scan Time: the lapsed time between a sound module's reception of a trigger signal to its reading the waveform amplitude to determine the volume (velocity) of a sound; measured in milliseconds

Crosstalk: the vibration of the drum or pad being struck to cause another drum trigger or pad to sound; usually caused by sympathetic vibrations

Double Trigger: one or more patches sounding after the initial (intended) pad or trigger hit

Threshold: the point below which a trigger waveform will not be recognized

Now that the terminology is out of the way, let's look at the physical setup needed to trigger acoustic drums.

The Setup

There is a myriad of different options for both drum triggers and trigger interfaces/sound modules. But have no fear—I'm here to help you understand what's needed to trigger drums.

Look at fig. 11.2. It is the most basic trigger setup and contains three items: the drum, the drum trigger mounted on the drum, and the trigger interface (in this case, a drum module). There are two different types of trigger interfaces: those that have sounds on board (often referred to as drum modules) and those without sounds (often referred to as trigger-to-MIDI converters). They both do the same thing—turn a trigger pulse into MIDI. Fig. 11.3 shows the setup for a trigger-to-MIDI converter and an external sound module. If you have an electronic drum set, you already have a drum module, the most expensive part of a drum trigger setup. How cool is that? If you don't have any kind of trigger-to-MIDI interface or drum module, I would suggest getting a drum module. A drum module is not only the trigger-to-MIDI interface, but it contains the sounds you'll be triggering.

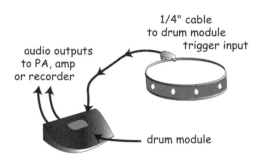

Fig. 11.2

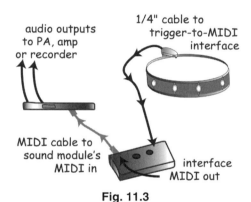

Fig. 11.3

If you already have an external sound module, you need only a trigger-to-MIDI interface. A trigger-to-MIDI interface doesn't have any sounds onboard. It will have to be connected to an external sound module with a MIDI cord. Roland's TMC-6 is about the size of a paperback book and its user interface is very friendly. The triggering is derivative of the TD-Series drum modules, so it's very quick and sophisticated.

Tip:
The TMC-6 can be used to expand the number of inputs on your existing drum module. Simply connect the MIDI out of the TMC-6 to the MIDI in on any drum module.

How Triggers Work

Stated plainly, triggers sense vibration from one of three places: drectly from the head, from the rim, or from the drum shell. Beyond that, there are two basic trigger construction types: those that stick to the head or shell with an adhesive (head-contact triggers) and those that use some sort of housing to mount to the rim and then press the trigger assembly against the head (rim-mount triggers). All of these triggers use piezo crystal technology. Piezo technology isn't some big mystery. We have piezo crystals all around us daily. Any piece of electronics that beeps, like a microwave, is probably using a piezo crystal as a speaker. When a piezo crystal has voltage applied to it, it vibrates, creating the beep sound. In drum trigger land, the crystal is being used in the opposite direction. When we hit the drum, the head (or shell) motion vibrates the piezo and a small amount of voltage is created and sent to the trigger interface. The trigger interface turns this voltage spike into MIDI information (note number, velocity, MIDI channel, etc.), and the MIDI information is sent to make the sound-source play the lick.

The Head-Contact Trigger

There are a number of drum trigger manufacturers, most of whom sell head contact triggers (see fig. 11.4). These are generally the least-expensive drum triggers available, but they're also the most fragile. Because they permanently mount to the head with adhesive or double-stick tape, they stay on the drum most of the time. As you can see, the

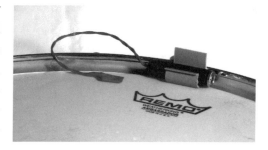

Fig. 11.4

sensor, exposed wire, and jack arrangement leaves it open to damage, most often pinching off the wire where it passes over the rim. Don't get me wrong—many professional drummers still use this kind of trigger. They work great, but you have to take care of them.

The Rim-Mount Trigger

Another trigger arrangement to surface in the last ten years or so is the rim-mount trigger. The major players are Roland and Trigger Perfect. Rim-mount triggers offer great performance and durability. Both Roland and Trigger Perfect have models to cover most needs. These drum triggers use a standard guitar cable (1/4" to 1/4") to connect to the drum module or trigger-to-MIDI interface. Fig. 11.5 shows the Roland RT-10K drum trigger.

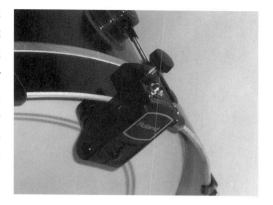

Fig. 11.5

Setting the Sound Module's Parameters

Practical application of triggering technology can be challenging at times—sort of like herding cats. But through patience and experimentation, it can be harnessed with great success. You have to remember: every drum is different. Between drum brands, drum sizes, heads, tuning, and playing styles, no two drums are alike. Because of that, there isn't just one set of software settings that will work on every drum. Believe me, I really wish there was because it would have made my last 15 years a bit easier.

Let's look at what each of the most common trigger settings (parameters) actually does. Different manufacturers may call the same function by different names, but they will operate similarly. Be sure to read the owner's manual for the interface or drum module you have. Familiarize yourself with your drum module's user interface. Yes, you should actually read the manual.

Trigger Type

Before any other parameter is set on the trigger interface, check to see if you can select the trigger type on your drum module or interface. While older modules may not have this parameter, most new ones—such as the Roland TD-Series modules—do. Choosing the trigger type will place the trigger settings in the ballpark of where they need to be.

Sensitivity and Gain

Next, the sensitivity level (or gain) must be set to match your playing style. Don't be afraid to hit the drums. Keep in mind, when you're by yourself setting trigger parameters, there's a tendency to play softer than you do in actual performance. Smack them! When you play your hardest, the sensitivity graph should just be peaking out. Avoid setting the sensitivity too high because it'll limit your dynamic range and can lead to problems like double triggering dropouts. If the triggering isn't very good at this point, fret not. We'll make it better.

Threshold

Threshold is next. I begin by setting the threshold parameter to zero, its most sensitive. Then I play the drum at the lowest volume I'll be performing and raise the threshold until the triggered sound begins to drop out occasionally. Now I lower the threshold a number or two. Note that your tendency will be to play the drum softer than you will in performance, so be realistic with your expectations.

Mask Time

Mask time is one of the most important parameters. Depending on the manufacturer, this setting has other names, so check the manual to see what it's called on your interface. Mask time is the parameter that is mainly responsible for getting rid of double, multiple, and false triggers. If possible, find out how your interface's numeric values correspond to actual milliseconds. This will make setting this parameter a bit clearer. If not, you'll just have to rely on your ear a bit more.

Take the mask time parameter all the way down to zero, then play the drum as fast you will in actual performance. Raise the mask time setting until the double triggering is gone. Next, continue to increase the value until some notes are not triggering, then back down the setting a few notches. Repeat this process for each drum.

For reference, the space between notes in a buzz or orchestral roll is about 15 ms. The space between flams is about 50 ms. As a rough rule of thumb, the snare will have the shortest mask time, the toms will have mask times that increase as the toms get lower in pitch, and the kick drum can have a mask time of 50 ms or more.

Trigger Wisdom/Conclusion

After following the directions above, it's possible that there still may be either note dropouts or double triggering. Such is life in triggering land. Here's where you must snatch the rock from my hand, Grasshopper. All I can say is play with the mask time, threshold, and sensitivity. It's a balancing act. There are no hard and fast rules at this point. You must experiment and tweak. You may even find that other trigger type settings work even better than the acoustic trigger setting.

If all else fails, you can muffle the snare and toms a bit. I often use one-third of a muffle ring on the snare drum and a small loop of gaffer's tape on the batter head of the toms. I've even seen people trigger drums that are filled with packing peanuts so that the drums make no acoustic sound at all. The more muffled the drum, the easier it is to trigger.

I hope this gives you some insight into the scary and mystical world of drum triggering. Dive in and experiment. It's extremely hard to make smoke come out of a drum module just by pushing buttons!

GLOSSARY

+4 db level
The output level used by professional, line-level audio gear. If it has RCA or 1/4" outputs, it's probably a +4 line-level output.

1/4" jack
The 1/4 female connector that receives the 1/4" male plug; also wired tip (+) and sleeve (−). Jacks are most often found on electronic instruments like guitars or synthesizers.

1/4" plug
Generally referred to as a guitar cord. It consists of two conductors, the tip (+) and the sleeve (−). It is a male connector and is most often used for line-level audio.

−10 db level
The output level used by consumer audio gear such as stereos. It generally uses outputs and inputs.

60-cycle hum
An unwanted low hum that sometimes can be heard in audio. It can be caused by improper grounding of AC power or by a faulty audio cord. In severe instances, getting rid of it may require smudging, or a ceremony involving a chicken.

AES/EBU
A digital audio input and output protocol from the Audio Engineering Society that is used on high-end professional audio gear.

amplitude

The height of a waveform. It is measured from the null point (where the wave crosses zero) to the peak of the wave. Above the null is +, below the null is −.

bit

A single digit of binary code, either zero or one, on or off.

byte

Eight bits make a byte. A byte can represent 256 distinct numbers in Base 10.

CD-R

A recordable CD. May be used to record files from a hard drive or create an audio CD for playback on CD players and/or computers. This format can be written only one time. Also known as "write once, read many."

CD-RW

Similar to a CD-R, but may be erased and re-written numerous times.

controller

An input device used to translate real time performance into MIDI data. This data is used to control other MIDI devices.

COSM

An acronym for Composite Object Sound Modeling. This is a type of sound design takes sampling to the next level.

crosstalk

Also known as trigger interaction. An unwanted trigger pulse generated by vibrations from a nearby source of sound, such as an adjacent drum, cymbal, heavier-than-average bass player, or loud monitor.

DIF-AT

A hardware interface device used to translate Roland's R-BUS protocol to Tascam and Lightpipe digital audio protocols, and visa versa.

double trigger

An unwanted note sounding after an initial strike, most often associated with acoustic drum triggering. Sympathetic vibrations resulting from an acoustic drum's long ring most often cause double triggering.

drum modeling

A term used to describe drum modules that use "modeling" technology, such as Roland's COSM. Also see COSM.

ethernet

A high-speed networking protocol for computers.

firewire

A high-speed communication protocol originally developed by Apple Computer. It is now being adopted by the music industry (under various names) as a new standard for digital audio and MIDI transfer. It is also used by computers to communicate with hard drives, CD/DVD-RW drives, and DV camcorders.

gain

Similar to the volume control on a stereo. This parameter is used to level out (equalize) the varying trigger pulse voltages from different manufacturers.

hard-disk recorder

Hardware and/or software used to record audio to hard disk or CD, instead of either analog or digital tape. May be stand-alone (such as Roland's VS-2480) or computer-based (such as Digital Performer and an audio interface).

lightpipe

A fiber optical interface protocol used on some hard-disk recorders to transfer digital audio.

line level

The level of output usually associated with synthesizers. Commonly uses a 1/4" male plug.

loop

A piece of audio or MIDI that plays repeatedly, end-to-end. Loops tend to be primarily drums and/or percussion, but may be other instruments, such as guitar.

mask time

The time a controller (trigger interface) will not allow another trigger pulse on the same input to be recognized. Measured in milliseconds from when a trigger pulse is first received. For reference: the individual hits of "orchestral" or "buzz" rolls are about 15–20 ms apart; fast tom notes are greater than 35 ms; quick kick drum doubles are greater than 48 ms. This parameter is used to eliminate double triggering.

mic connector

See XLR connector.

mic level

The level of output usually associated with microphones. Commonly uses an XLR connector.

MIDI

An acronym for Musical Instrument Digital Interface. A common communication standard for music electronics agreed upon by all manufacturers. The spec has 16 MIDI channels. Most values (such as velocity) are in increments of one, with values from 0–127 (1–128).

MIDI cord

The five-pin DIN cord used to connect one MIDI device to another.

MIDI interface

A hardware device that plugs into a computer and translates MIDI data into a format that the computer can understand.

MIDI velocity

The steps (increments) of volume used by MIDI. The specification calls for a value range from 0–127; the lower the value, the softer the sound. A value of 127 results in the loudest volume a sound can be played. Different drums have different perceived velocity requirements. For example, snare drums need a wide velocity range, toms a little narrower range, and kick drums a very limited range, generally only three or four volume levels. This information is sent out with note number information within the MIDI data stream.

MIDI volume

Used in conjunction with MIDI Velocity. MIDI Volume controls the overall loudness of a sound independent of Velocity. MIDI Volume is MIDI channel dependent. It affects all sounds responding to the MIDI channel it is transmitted on.

millisecond

A unit of time. One second=1000 milliseconds (ms). Sound in air travels approximately one foot per millisecond. For example, if you are seated at a drum set, sound from striking a snare drum takes about two or three milliseconds to reach your ear.

MotU

Short for "Mark of the Unicorn," a manufacturer of sequencing and digital audio software and hardware for both Macintosh and Windows computers. *http://motu.com*

multi-timbral

The ability of a synth, sampler and/or sound module to play more than one type or groups of sound simultaneously; for example: guitar, keyboard, bass, and drum sounds. These are often on their own individual MIDI channels.

piezo element

A ceramic crystal that gives off an electrical pulse when it is put in motion (struck). The opposite is also true: when electricity is applied to a piezo element, it vibrates. Most beeps in electronic devices today use a piezo element as a speaker. Most drum pads use piezo technology.

polyphonic

The ability for a synth and/or sampler to have multiple voices sound at the same time. See Polyphony.

polyphony

The number of voices a synth and/or sampler can play at one time before a voice is dropped. The dropped voice is most often the first voice played.

R-BUS

A proprietary interface used by Roland® to transfer digital audio and other information between devices.

RCA connector

A two-conductor connector used for analog audio as well as SPIDIF digital connections.

rise time

The time it takes for a trigger pulse to reach its peak (full amplitude). This time relates to the "scan time" parameter in the trigger input settings of most drum modules. It is measured in milliseconds (ms). One second=1000 ms.

S/PDIF

An acronym for the Sony-Phillips Digital Interface Format digital connection.

sampling

The act of making a digital representation of an analog sound.

scan time

The amount of time a trigger interface (controller) microprocessor looks at a received trigger pulse before it reads the waveform amplitude. This parameter is measured in milliseconds, with a usable range between zero and four ms. This parameter is automatically set when a pad type is selected in the trigger settings area.

sensitivity

Acts like a volume control. It is used to adjust a pad or drum trigger to match the player's strike intensity.

sequencer

A device, most often software-based, used to record MIDI performances. The sequencer records MIDI data, not sound.

sound module

This most often refers to a rack-mount or a table-top style of synthesizer or drum module. It less often refers to synthesizers that have built-in keyboards called "keyboard controllers" or "workstations."

spike

The top (peak) of a trigger pulse. Also see amplitude and waveform.

standard MIDI file

A cross-platform MIDI file format that adheres to the GM (General MIDI) specification. It will open on all sequencing software, and will play back correctly on any GM sound module, hardware, or software.

surge protector

A device used to protect electronic gear from harmful voltage spikes.

sys ex dump

Short for "system exclusive dump." Used to describe the process by which all sound modules settings can be saved to an external MIDI sequencer or sound librarian software.

system exclusive dump

See Sys Ex Dump.

threshold

The point at which, when crossed, a trigger pulse will be recognized by a trigger input.

trigger

A device, generally based on a piezo element, that is plugged into the trigger input of a drum module or trigger-to-MIDI interface. It most often is a shorthand way of referring to an acoustic drum trigger.

trigger input

The place on drum modules and trigger-to-MIDI converters into which external trigger devices such as drum triggers and pads are plugged. It may also refer to the pulse that is generated when a pad or an acoustic drum trigger is hit.

trigger interface

A controller that has inputs in which to plug external trigger devices, like drum pads. Most interfaces referred to by this name do not have sounds onboard. They just transmit MIDI data from trigger input.

trigger pulse

The electricity given off by a trigger device when it is struck.

USB

Universal Serial Bus. This bus type is found on many computers and is used to communicate to MIDI interfaces and other external computer devices.

velocity curve

The curve of a sound volume's (MIDI velocity) change in relation to the change in stick velocity. Default curve is linear (1:1) in all Roland drum modules. Other curves include logarithmic, exponential, and variations.

wave

See waveform.

waveform

The visual shape of a trigger pulse. It is plotted as amplitude in volts vs. time in milliseconds.

XLR

A three-conductor connector generally used for mic-level audio connections. Also is used for AES/EBU connections.

ABOUT THE AUTHOR

You may not know it, but you've heard Mike Snyder's work. For ten years he was a regular on the Los Angeles recording scene, bringing his special talents to many film and television soundtracks. In addition to every Mel Brooks movie from *Spaceballs* to *Robin Hood: Men in Tights*, his playing may be heard on many popular syndicated television shows, including *Home Improvement*, *Dinosaurs*, and *The Little Mermaid*. His recording work now focuses on jingles, library music, music for industrial video, and lots of drum and percussion loops.

Returning to the sanity of the Northwest after ten years of L.A. session work and life in Southern California, Mike continues to develop his unique talents. His varied performance abilities—which include drum set, percussion, and extensive electronic knowledge—keep Mike busy recording, creating drum loops, and giving drum clinics in the U.S. and abroad. Mike holds a Bachelor's degree in percussion from The University of Oregon and a Master's degree in percussion from The University of Southern California. He is the author of *Linear Drumming: Creative Practice*, published by Drumbz Publications (2nd edition 12/2006), and is a frequent columnist for *DRUM!* magazine. His continued album tracking, industrial, and national jingle work as a drummer, programmer, hand percussionist, and composer include HP, Dupont, Microsoft, Westin Hotels, and Nike.

In addition to his performing, Mike has been heavily involved in electronic percussion design since the mid-1980s. *DRUM!* magazine's "Drummies" readers' poll named him runner-up electronic drummer of 2003. Because of his direction-setting designs for Trigger Perfect drum triggers and his continued work with Roland Drums and Percussion, his ideas and designs continue to influence the direction of electronic drums and percussion.

INDEX